MW00995773

THE 5-INGREDIENT KETO CROCK POT COOKBOOK

Easy & Healthy Ketogenic Crock Pot Recipes For The Everyday Home

© Copyright 2017 - All rights reserved.

The contents of this book may not be reproduced, duplicated or transmitted without direct written permission from the author.

Under no circumstances will any legal responsibility or blame be held against the publisher for any reparation, damages, or monetary loss due to the information herein, either directly or indirectly.

Legal Notice:
This book is copyright protected. This is only for personal use. You cannot amend, distribute, sell, use, quote or paraphrase any part or the content within this book without the consent of the author.

Disclaimer Notice:
Please note the information contained within this document is for educational and entertainment purposes only. Every attempt has been made to provide accurate, up to date and reliable complete information. No warranties of any kind are expressed or implied. Readers acknowledge that the author is not engaging in the rendering of legal, financial, medical or professional advice. The content of this book has been derived from various sources. Please consult a licensed professional before attempting any techniques outlined in this book.

By reading this document, the reader agrees that under no circumstances are is the author responsible for any losses, direct or indirect, which are incurred as a result of the use of information contained within this document, including, but not limited to, —errors, omissions, or inaccuracies.

Table of Contents

Introduction

Losing weight, feeling great, thinking clearly, and increasing focus... These are all benefits of the Ketogenic diet, which is taking the world by storm. This book is going to teach you exactly how you can follow the Ketogenic diet and experience all of the benefits that come along with it.

But there is more...

In this book you are also going to learn all about the Crock Pot, how to use it, how to convert your favorite meals to Crock Pot meals and how the Crock Pot can help you stick to the Ketogenic diet.

I'm not done yet...

At the end of this book you are going to find tons of five ingredient easy Ketogenic friendly recipes that you can make right in your Crock Pot! All of these recipes are delicious and simple. You can make them in almost no time at all and they are going to help ensure that when mealtime comes, you don't find yourself tempted to grab that processed junk which is not going to benefit your body at all.

What are you waiting for? Let's get started learning all about the Ketogenic diet and how you can make it work for you.

Chapter 1: What is the Ketogenic Diet?

The Ketogenic diet is a low carb diet, much like the Paleo diet or the Atkins diet. The idea of the diet is for a person to get the majority of the calories from protein as well as fat instead of from carbohydrates. You will eliminate foods such as bread, pastries, soda, and sugar.

When you are following the Ketogenic diet, you will eat less than 50 grams of carbohydrates each day. This is going to make your body run out of fuel after about three to four days. At this point, your body is going to start breaking down fat and protein. This, of course, is going to cause weight loss. Once your body reaches this point, it has reached ketosis.

Who Uses the Ketogenic Diet?

Most of the time, people who want to lose weight are the ones that use the Ketogenic diet however, it is also used for managing some medical issues such as epilepsy, acne, diseases of the brain and even heart diseases. If you are suffering from any type of diseases, you will want to make sure that you consult with your doctor before starting the Ketogenic diet. It is extremely important for you to talk to your doctor before starting the Ketogenic diet if you have diabetes.

The Ketogenic diet is going to make you lose a lot more weight in the first six months than most other diets will. The reason for this is because your body has to burn more calories in order to turn fat to energy than it does when it turns carbohydrates into energy. Some people also believe that when a person eats a high-protein and high-fat diet, he or she feels more satisfied and eats less, however, more studies need to be done before this is proven.

The Ketogenic diet burns through insulin very quickly which ensures that your body does not store it. This means that your body is going to start making less insulin because it is not going to need as much insulin. Having lower levels of insulin in the body might help to reduce your chances of developing certain cancers. It is also believed that the Ketogenic diet can slow the rate at which cancer spreads, however, more research is needed to determine how this actually works.

When your body reaches the state of ketosis, it becomes a fat burning machine. This also means that your body can turn the fat that is in your liver into energy which will specifically fuel your brain.

There are different versions or types of Ketogenic diets. There is the standard Ketogenic diet which when followed, you will get 75 percent of your calories from fat, 20 percent from protein and 5 percent from carbohydrates.

When you are following the cyclical Ketogenic diet, you will follow the regular Ketogenic diet for 5 days then for 2 days, you will follow a high carb diet.

The targeted Ketogenic diet allows you to increase your carbohydrate intake before or after your workouts.

Finally, there is the high protein Ketogenic diet which is pretty close to the standard Ketogenic diet, however, when you follow the high protein Ketogenic diet, you will increase the amount of protein that you eat to 35 percent of your calories and the amount of fat that you will drop to 60 percent of the calories that you eat each day while the percentage of carbohydrates will remain the same at 5 percent of your daily caloric intake.

It is important to know that the high-protein and standard Ketogenic diet are the only versions that have ever been studied. The cyclical and the targeted Ketogenic diet are generally only used by athletes or bodybuilders. Therefore, this book is going to focus on the standard Ketogenic diet. If you would like to try the high-protein Ketogenic diet, you will simply follow the guidelines previously given.

One of the things that people love most about the Ketogenic diet is that they are able to lose up to 2 times more weight than they would if they followed a low-fat calorie-restricted diet. There are no counting calories and you never have to go hungry.

The reason that the weight loss is improved is that when you reach the state of ketosis, your blood sugar levels are lowered. When the blood sugar levels are naturally lowered and kept at a stable level a person will lose more weight.

What Can You Eat?

Many people are quite surprised at some of the foods that they can eat when they are on the ketogenic diet because these are foods that most diets will tell you to avoid.

- *Red meat* is a food that many diets will tell you to eat in moderation, however, when you follow the Ketogenic diet, you will be basing your meals around a lot of red meat as well as poultry such as chicken or turkey.
- *Fish* is a common diet food, however, when you follow the Ketogenic diet you will want to focus on eating fatty fish such as trout, salmon, mackerel, or tuna.
- *Eggs* are another food that many people have been taught to avoid if they want to eat healthily or lose weight however when you are following the Ketogenic diet you will want to eat farm fresh eggs or omega-3 eggs. Another great thing, you get to eat the entire egg, not just the white.
- *Cream and butter* are full of fat and for that reason, they are often avoided by those that want to lose weight, however, they are another food that you will want to make sure you are eating when you are following the Ketogenic diet.
- We all know that *nuts and seeds* are great for us but we are also told to eat them in moderation because of the amount of fat that they contain. When you are following the Ketogenic diet, feel free to eat all of the nuts and seeds you can handle.
- *Healthy fats and oils* are a very important part of the Ketogenic diet. While you will want to avoid fats such as vegetable oils, you will want to use coconut oil, EVOO, and avocado oil in place of vegetable oil.
- *Cheese* should be unprocessed however, this is a great food that you can eat while you are following the Ketogenic diet. Focus on eating mozzarella, cream cheese, blue cheese, goat cheese, or cheddar.
- *Avocados* are a very important part of this diet. They are a wonderful replacement for condiments that you will no longer be eating such as mayonnaise; you can eat them plain, or make guacamole out of them.
- When it comes to vegetables you will focus on eating *low-carb vegetables*, such as onions, peppers, tomatoes and almost all green vegetables.
- The *condiments* that you will use are going to be limited therefore you will want to season your food with salt, pepper, as well as other herbs and spices.

Foods You Must Avoid

There are many great foods that you can eat while you are on the Ketogenic diet, however, like all other diets, there are certain foods that you must avoid.

- **Grains and starches** such as pasta, rice, wheat-based items, and cereal should not be eaten if you are following the Ketogenic diet.
- **Sugary foods** such as smoothies, ice cream, cake, cookies, fruit juice, candy, soda, or other sweet sugary foods must be avoided in order for you to reach a state of ketosis.
- **Fruit** is avoided except for berries; however, the berries must be eaten in small portions.
- Just like if you were following the Paleo diet, when you are on the Ketogenic diet, you should avoid **legumes or beans** such as kidney beans, chickpeas, peas, lentils, and all other beans.
- While a person is on the Ketogenic diet they can eat a lot of fat, and what you cannot eat is **unhealthy fat** such as mayonnaise or processed vegetable oils, or any other unhealthy fat.
- Potatoes, carrots, sweet potatoes, and all other **tubers or root vegetables** will be avoided when you are following the Ketogenic diet.
- There are going to be some **sauces** that are going to be off limits as well as **condiments**. It is important to check the ingredients of your sauces and condiments to ensure that they are allowed. If a sauce or condiment contains sugar or unhealthy fat, you will want to avoid it.
- You will completely avoid all diet products including **foods that claim to be low fat**. These types of foods are highly processed. Most of the time these foods will contain high amounts of sugar (because sugar is actually fat-free) or they will be high in carbohydrates.
- One issue that many people have with the Ketogenic diet is that they are not able to drink **alcohol** because it contains so many carbohydrates. If you drink alcohol while on the Ketogenic diet, you will not be able to reach a state of ketosis. If you have already reached this state, the alcohol will throw you out of it.
- No **"sugar-free" foods** are allowed. Most of us have seen the sugar-free versions of our favorite foods on the shelves at the grocery store and many people think that these would be great to eat when you are following any diet. The problem is that these foods are highly processed and they are packed full of chemicals, which will stop you from reaching a state of ketosis. On top of that, you don't want to be filling your body full of chemicals.

9

Benefits of the Ketogenic Diet

The Ketogenic diet was created in the early 1920's in order to improve the health of those that were struggling with on specific issues of the brain, however, researchers found that it helped in many other ways as well.

Most of us know that fasting, both long-term and short-term is not always feasible, even though it does come with many benefits. Even so, we are not supposed to fast for more than a day or two at the most. When we do fast, we have to be very careful and we need to only fast when we are being supervised by our doctor.

It was because of this issue with fasting that the Ketogenic diet was created. This diet will mimic the effects that you would get if you were fasting while still allowing you to eat certain foods. The Ketogenic diet also ensures that your body does not suffer the negative effects of not getting enough calories for an extended period of time.

Today we hear people talking about Keto. But what is it? Keto is nothing more than a shortened version of the word Ketogenic or ketosis.

When the body reaches the state of ketosis, the liver will release fats that are known as ketones. These ketones are going to burn fat better than carbs which will create a balanced environment inside of the body. This then helps to reduce weight and improve overall health.

In short, if we eat fewer carbohydrates and more foods that contain healthy fats along with a moderate amount of protein, our body will reach the state of ketosis. When this happens, our energy is going to come from the ketone instead of glucose. You see, most people live with their bodies in the glycolytic state. In other words, they are getting most of their energy from sugar.

Once the body has reached the state of ketosis, the body is going to start burning fat instead of carbohydrates, which will result in rapid weight loss, even though the person is consuming a large amount of fat and enough calories.

Of course, there are many other benefits of the Ketogenic diet besides reaching a state of ketosis and they include:

1. Finally reaching that healthy weight. Diets like the Ketogenic diet have been used for years to help people lose weight. When I say like the Ketogenic diet, I mean diets that focus on low-carb, moderate-protein, and high-fat intake. One of the reasons that the appetite is reduced when eating a high-fat diet is because of the satiating nature of foods that are high fat. Also, when you eat a high fat and low -carb diet, your body is naturally going to start using the fat that it has stored as a source of energy. This means that your body is going to start finally tapping into those fat reserves and using them up. This will result in dramatic weight loss.

2. The Ketogenic diet is a great way for you to get your blood sugar balanced. It is a great diet for those that want to maintain balanced blood sugar (if the blood sugar levels are already normal) and for those that are pre-diabetic and suffering from diabetes. Studies have proven that when a person eats a low-carb diet, which will reduce the amount of sugar and grain that a person eats, the body naturally begins to balance the blood sugar. You do not have to worry about your blood sugar levels spiking or dropping any longer because you will not be eating any artificial or processed sugars.

3. If you want a healthy brain than the Ketogenic diet might be for you even if you are not interested in burning fat by using the Ketogenic diet. One of the main reasons that so many people love the Ketogenic diet is because the diet helps to support brain function as well as a healthy brain. In fact, the diet is becoming very popular with those that work in high-performance fields because of this. In one study that was done on old rats, it was found that the Ketogenic diet helped to boost their cognitive performance. There are of course more studies being done however, the outcome looks promising. Many people are even suggesting the Ketogenic diet could help to prevent or reverse Alzheimer's disease. If you know a person who has followed the Ketogenic diet and want proof of how much it helps the brain just ask them. Chances are, they are going to tell you that they think more clearly and their mind works much better.

4. So many people today are suffering from gut health issues but did you know that a lot of these issues are caused by the overconsumption of carbohydrates? Yet, most of those that have these gut issues shudder when they think about eating a low-carb, high-fat diet. The reason for this is because when we increase our fat intake, we can also increase the time that it takes for our food to leave our bodies after entering it. However, this is most often a side effect that only lasts a very short period of time. Of course, more studies need to be done to determine exactly how

the Ketogenic diet helps to improve digestive health however, it is a great way to start supporting your gut healthy now.

5. Inflammation is a huge problem for many people right now. So many people are suffering from inflammation and what we are learning is that it is this inflammation that is causing many diseases. The problem is, while inflammation can cause damage to your health, you also can't live without it. Most of us have heard of anti-inflammatory medicine, anti-inflammatory foods, or even the anti-inflammatory diet but do we really understand what inflammation is?

In short, inflammation is how the body responses to threats such as toxic chemicals, infection or even stress. You see, when our immune system senses that there is a danger, proteins are activated. The job of these proteins is to protect our cells and tissue within the body. Inflammation is actually good and it serves our bodies, however, it is when our immune systems begin overreacting that can be dangerous. This is when the inflammation begins causing problems because instead of attacking the treats such as infection, it begins attacking our bodies. This is known as chronic inflammation and can happen for many reasons such as an autoimmune disorder, chronic stress, or eating too many sugary foods.

Inflammation is most helpful to our bodies when we are fighting an infection, illness, or when we have a wound. Inflammation is the reason that your glands in your throat swell when you are suffering from a sore throat. It is the reason that a cut becomes red and warm. These are all signs that your immune system is doing what it is supposed to do, sending the white blood cells where they are needed. This makes inflammation a vital function for our bodies however the problems come when the illness or infection is gone but the inflammation stays.

Inflammation can cause gut issues, actually attacking the digestive tract and resulting in a disease called inflammatory bowel disease. This can cause cramps, diarrhea, ulcers, and it can also result in the removal of a person's intestines.

Too much inflammation can also cause damage to your joints resulting in rheumatoid arthritis. It can cause heart disease or even a heart attack. It has also been found that chronic inflammation is linked to many different types of cancer as well. Chronic inflammation can cause you to be unable to sleep, cause problems with the lungs such as COPD, asthma, or recurrent infections.

It can also cause periodontal disease, which has been linked to heart disease as well as dementia. It damages a person's bones, makes it all but impossible to lose weight, can cause skin issues such as psoriasis, and it has even been linked to mental disorders such as depression.

The Ketogenic diet has been shown to reduce the discomfort that is caused by chronic inflammation as well as reduce the inflammation in the body and help restore a healthy inflammation response within the body.

What many people find shocking when it comes to the Ketogenic diet is that they are able to maintain high levels of energy throughout the day. There are no more afternoon slumps, no more needs to hit the vending machine for a sugar rush, and no more energy drinks. Because of that, there are also no more crashes.

How could this be possible? This happens because of the ketones that are produced from the fat that the person is eating. The fat is a great source of fuel for the body and once someone has reached the state of ketosis, they are going to find that they can go for hours without eating and they will have no shift in the amount of energy that they have.

Of course, those are just a few benefits of the Ketogenic diet. It is important that you only use the Ketogenic diet after speaking to your doctor and getting their approval. There are a few other warnings that you should be made aware of as well before trying the diet.

Warnings

While there are many reasons that people go on the Ketogenic diet, there are a few things that will remain the same for everyone. Everyone who goes on the Ketogenic diet is going to be eating a small amount of carbohydrates, much more fat than they are used to and it is likely that they will be eating more protein as well. It is very important for you to speak to your doctor before going on the Ketogenic diet because while it is a great diet there are some risks.

We have already learned that when a person is following the Ketogenic diet, their body is going to use fat for energy instead of carbohydrates. When you first begin the diet, your body is going to have to adjust to using this fat instead of carbohydrates as fuel. If you jump into the diet too quickly or if your body has a hard time adjusting to it, it is possible for you to suffer from fatigue, low blood sugar levels, and headaches. Of course, these effects are only temporary and will go away once your body reaches the state of ketosis. If you want to avoid these side effects I suggest that you begin by making small changes in your diet.

You can begin by cutting out certain foods such as sugary sweets and increasing the number of low carbohydrate vegetables that you eat. Then move on to cutting out grains and so forth. This is going to allow your body to ease into the diet and you will not suffer from any of the aforementioned side effects.

When you are following the Ketogenic diet, you have to understand that you may suffer from acidosis. When your body reaches a state of ketosis, it is going to become more acidic because ketones are acid. The good news is that your body is very good at adapting to this new state and it should begin producing more bicarbonate in order to ensure that your body does not become too acidic.

However, it is still important for you to make sure that you are checking the acidity of your blood on a regular basis because if it does become too acidic, you can suffer from bone damage and kidney stones. It is very easy to manage acidosis, simply drink some water with bicarbonate soda added to it. However, this should be done under the supervision of a doctor. You should never attempt to control the acid levels in your blood without the advice of a doctor.

As I just mentioned, it is possible to develop kidney stones while you are following the Ketogenic diet. This is a rare side effect but it does happen to between 3 and 10 percent of people who follow the Ketogenic diet. It is more likely that you will develop kidney stones if you are taking topiramate or zonisamide which are common medications for epilepsy. Dehydration also increases your chances of developing kidney stones. Therefore, it is important for you to not only manage acidosis as talked about in the previous paragraph but to ensure you are drinking plenty of water as well.

One very annoying side effect of the Ketogenic diet is constipation. The constipation is not usually dangerous and occurs because the Ketogenic diet is low in fiber while high in fat. You can manage this by increasing the amount of water that you drink and by eating a lot of foods that are high in fiber but low in carbohydrates such as chia seeds, flaxseed, hemp powder, or leafy greens. If you have to, you can also use stool softeners.

Finally, it is important for you to know that this diet can cause some nutrient deficiencies because of the restrictions. When you are following this diet, you are not always going to be able to meet your mineral and vitamin needs, therefore, it is important that you take a supplement. It is also important that you are eating plenty of foods that are packed full of nutrients such as nuts, avocados, seeds, and coconut oil. A simple daily vitamin should be fine however, it is still important to have your nutrient levels checked on a regular basis. This will ensure that if you are deficient your doctor will be able to provide you with a stronger supplement of just what you need.

While the Ketogenic diet does have some side effects and those that do not understand the diet have tried to convince everyone that it is not safe to follow, the truth is, the diet is completely safe. That is if you follow it under the supervision of a doctor. You should never try to follow this diet without speaking to your doctor first and without regular checkups to ensure that you are not causing more harm to your body. There are certain health issues that will also have to be monitored such as diabetes so always make sure you discuss any diet with your doctor before you begin it.

Case study

Ketogenic diet and Schizophrenia

One study was done where it was found that longstanding schizophrenic symptoms were resolved after the patient began the Ketogenic diet. This study was done by BioMed Central Ltd in 2008 and published in 2009.

After a review of the results, it was concluded that it was possible that the elimination of gluten from the diet had resolved the disease.

The report

The patient was a 70-year-old white female who had been diagnosed with schizophrenia when she was just 17. The diagnosis was based on her hallucinations, disorganized speech, and her paranoia.

The patient had reported visual hallucinations as well as hearing voices. She stated that she had seen skeletons and that the voices would often tell her to hurt herself. According to the patient, she had seen the hallucinations and heard the voices on a regular basis, almost daily since she was seven-years-old.

The patient had been hospitalized no less than five times over a six-year period due to attempting suicide and suffering from an increase in psychotic symptoms. The woman had attempted to overdose on her medication, she had tried to cut herself, and she had ingested cleaning agents.

She had been hospitalized just five months prior to initiating the Ketogenic diet. She talked about her suicidal intentions as well as her hallucinations with her doctor who had tried to adjust her medications accordingly. Before the Ketogenic diet, she was taking 900 milligrams of lithium, 40 milligrams of ziprasidone, 30 milligrams of aripiprazole, 100 milligrams of lamotrigine, 900 milligrams of quetiapine and an unknown dosage of olanzapine.

Her other medical problems included depression, obesity, hypertension, gastroesophageal reflux disease, obstructive sleep apnea, glaucoma, urinary incontinence, trochanteric bursitis, a prior cholecystectomy and peripheral neuropathy. Her medications for these medical problems were 100 milligrams of atenolol, 20 milligrams of furosemide, 100 milligrams of trazodone, 100 milligrams of sertraline, 1 drop in each eye of brimonidine, one drop in each eye of timolol, and 400 IU of vitamin E every other day.

On a typical day, the patient would eat an egg and cheese sandwich, water, diet soda, pimento cheese, chicken salad, barbecued pork, macaroni and cheese, hamburger helper, and potatoes. She rated her fatigue as a three on a scale of zero to four with four being the worst. She weighed 310 pounds, giving her a BMI of 52.6. Her blood pressure was 130/72 and her pulse was 68 BPM.

When physically examined, it was shown that she was an obese female male that was disheveled and lacked hygiene, however, she was otherwise unremarkable.

The patient was introduced to the diet and told to follow the diet in which she could eat an unlimited amount of meat as well as eggs, 4 ounces of hard cheese, 1 cup of low-carb vegetables and 2 cups of salad vegetables each day. She was to eat no more than 20 grams of carbohydrates each day.

After following the diet for 7 days, the patient returned and stated that she was feeling well and had increased energy. She returned again 19 days after that and stated that she had seen no skeletons nor had she heard any voices. She had noticed this after only 8 days after she had started the diet. There had been no change in her medication.

The patient stated that she was not hungry and she was very happy that he no longer heard voices. She had lost 11 pounds; her blood pressure was 150/84 and her heart rate was 76 BPM.

Over a 12-month period, the patient continued to follow the diet. She weighed 288 pounds at the end of 12 months and stated that she had more energy. She did admit to having several non-compliant days in which she ate pasta, cakes, and break and she had 3 isolated episodes during that time. However, the hallucinations never returned.

In this study, there was a sudden resolution to schizophrenic symptoms that had been long standing when the patient was introduced to the Ketogenic diet, which is often used for weight loss. Previously it had been observed during WWII that when a patient was admitted to the hospital and the amount of bread that they ate was limited, the symptoms of schizophrenia were reduced which suggest that it is possible that bread could affect the disease. It was also found that in areas such as the South Pacific where the people rarely eat grains, there is a much lower rate of schizophrenia.

In the past, some researchers have linked celiac disease and schizophrenia, suggesting both are caused by consuming gluten. Today we find that when a person is treated for schizophrenia, they are usually treated with pharmaceutical medications. However, there have been several small studies such as the one just discussed that show the same results. When a person removes gluten from their diet, the symptoms of schizophrenia disappear.

In one study that was done, 10 percent of the patients that were suffering from schizophrenia saw their symptoms improve simply by eliminating gluten from their diet. Another study that was done, also showed, that when a person switched to the Ketogenic diet which is gluten-free, the symptoms of schizophrenia were reduced.

On top of this it was also shown that when a person ate a large amount of carbohydrates, it often leads to a psychotic episode. The Ketogenic diet also has a history of treating pediatric epilepsy, obesity, and heart disease.

At this time, more research is needed to confirm that gluten and schizophrenia are linked and that by eliminating gluten, schizophrenia can be eliminated. However, the outlook is good and this study suggests that if the elimination of gluten can reduce the symptoms of schizophrenia, it may be able to reduce the symptoms of other mental disorder such as depression.

Most of us know that what we eat affects every part of our being but many people forget this when it comes to their mental health. One patient, Jodi found this out when she was trying to lose weight.

She had suffered from depression for years and had accepted that she was going to have to take antidepressant medication. That was when she decided that she was going to try the Ketogenic diet. She needed to lose weight and was sure that in doing so, she would begin to feel better not just physically but mentally as well.

Within the first month of starting the diet, she had not only lost weight but she had lost her depression as well. She recalled that the diet changed everything, stating that it was as if a veil lifted and suddenly she could see everything clearly.

Jodi had found herself using the Ketogenic diet to lose weight but as a result, the depression disappeared. This is something that researchers are just starting to explore. Believe it or not, researchers are just starting to accept that what we eat affects our mental health. However, what they are finding is supporting that idea.

The quality of the food that you eat, how often you eat the foods, and how much of the food that you eat affects not just your physical health but your mental health as well. When a person who is suffering from mental disorders such as depression or anxiety eats a traditional diet, which contains gluten and other highly processed foods, they are unable to overcome the condition. However, when they switch to the Ketogenic diet or simply remove the gluten from their diet and focus on eating nutrient-dense foods, they find that the mental illness disappears.

Today there is a lot of hype when it comes to making sure that you are getting enough carbohydrates. We are told to eat plenty of whole grains. It is often suggested that we have whole grains with every meal. However, what is being left out is that it could be these whole grains that are causing the epidemic of mental disorders today.

If you suffer from a mental disorder or you have ever known someone that does then you know how hard life can be. You know that there are days when you simply can't get out of bed and you just don't feel like going on any longer. What if all of that could be cured simply by switching your diet? Of course, this is not going to work for everyone however, the research looks promising and it is definitely worth trying if you want to get off of the antidepressants or other medications and start living the life that you have always dreamed of.

One study that was done in 2013 that consuming sweets, gluten, or other processed foods while a woman is pregnant or breastfeeding, increases the chances of the child having a behavioral or mental health issue dramatically before the age of five.

Right now, researchers are unsure how the food that we eat relates to mental health issues however, it is obvious that there is a link. However, the problem is that they do not know if the food makes the mental illness that already existed worse or if it is the food that is causing the mental illness.

It is possible that mood disorders actually change depending on what a person eats but it is also possible that the mental disorder actually affects the way that a person eats.

Another woman changed her diet because she was suffering from gastrointestinal issues. She was also suffering from bipolar disorder but did not think changing her diet would help. When she tried the Ketogenic diet, she not only found relief from the gastrointestinal issues but suddenly she was no longer suffering from bipolar disorder either.

She said that it only took two days before she could tell that there was a change and that her mind felt clear for the first time in a very long time. While this may seem like a very quick turnaround time, studies have actually found that diet can impair the mind, memory, and attention in less than one week.

The woman was able to stop taking her medication and has had no episodes in over three years. She has tried to share her findings with doctors, neurologists, and psychiatrists all over the country; however, they are simply not interested in the findings. Why? It is important to know that these doctors get paid, they make their money when people are ill. It would be silly for them to put themselves out of business wouldn't it? The doctors get paid to treat ill people. If we can heal our bodies with the food that we eat, if we can stop suffering from ailments by changing our diets, we no longer have to be treated by a doctor.

The truth is, there is very little information out there about how the food that you eat affects your mental and physical health but every study that has ever been done has ended with the same result. When a person changes the way that they eat, they are able to get off the meds, stop suffering and start living the life that they have always wanted to live.

Ketogenic Tips and Tricks

Going on the Ketogenic diet is like going on a new adventure. However, for every adventure, we need to make sure that we have the right tips to ensure our success. These tips are not only going to help you succeed while following the Ketogenic diet but they are also going to ensure that you stay healthy along the way.

1. Take a chance with ghee. Chances are, you are going to love it. Of course, butter is great but try cooking your steak with ghee, you will never want to go back.

2. It is very important for you to take your Omega's seriously. It is vital to your health that you have more Omega-3's in your diet than Omega-6's. Since you are going to be consuming a lot of fat it is very easy for you to have too much Omega-6's in your diet. If this happens, the diet is going to do more harm than good. Take those Omega-3's.

3. Do not drink any alcohol while you are following the Ketogenic diet because this is going to stop any weight loss.

4. Cream cheese is not good for you. If you are going to use it in your recipes, it is likely that you are going to have to use a ton of it. The problem with this is that it does contain quite a bit of carbohydrates.

5. Whip up some heavy cream and peanut butter for a delicious and tasty mousse. Add a bit of stevia if you need it to be sweeter.

6. If you need something sweet, there are low carb chocolate chips that you can add to your favorite recipes.

7. If you need some whipped cream, look for the version that is made by Land O' Lakes. It is made with heavy cream, which means it has no carbohydrates in it.

8. Be careful when you are thinking about purchasing foods that are fat-free or sugar-free because they are still going to be packed full of carbohydrates.

9. Don't worry about purchasing anything low fat because when you are following the Ketogenic diet, you will want to ensure you are getting as much fat as possible. If

you are not getting enough fat in your diet, your body is going to convert the protein that you eat to sugar.

10. Do not start to by eating too much bacon when you begin the diet. Most people are super excited that they can eat as much bacon as they want on this diet, however, too much of a good thing is never good. Many people who report loving bacon before they started the diet, can't stand the smell of it after eating too much of it.

11. Make sure that you are actually digesting your food. Digestion starts with chewing. You will also want to make sure that you are drinking plenty of water. The broth recipes in this book are also going to aid with digestion. If you are not digesting properly, you are not going to lose weight.

12. You must drink a ton of water. Your body has to have a lot of water in order to function properly. Water is going to aid with digestion and it is going to boost your weight loss as well.

13. If you want to have a quick snack on hand, boil a dozen eggs. When they have cooled, peel them and then place them in a Ziplocs bag. They will be ready to eat when you want them. Of course, you can purchase pre-boiled and peeled eggs, however, most people prefer to use their money toward other foods when they are following the Ketogenic diet.

14. Make sure that you are eating 20 net carbs per day. What is a net carb? This is the total carbohydrate in your food minus the fiber.

Ketogenic Diet and Eating on the Go

It does not matter what diet you are following, you are going to find yourself in a situation where you need to eat but are unable to go home and cook your meal. Maybe you want to go out to dinner with your friends or family. Maybe you are just in a hurry, hungry, and have no time to cook. Or maybe you are hanging out with some friends and everyone wants to grab something to eat.

We have all found ourselves in that position. We have all found ourselves in a situation where we have been hungry, needed to eat, or wanted to eat and just can't take the time to cook.

What are you supposed to do when you are following the Ketogenic diet and don't have time to make your meal? I do suggest that you plan events like this ahead of time. For example, always take your lunch to work with you, make food to take with you to events such as local ball games and such. However, things happen and you cannot be prepared for everything. Plus, restaurants do not look highly upon those that bring their own food in.

The good news is that there are plenty of options for you. When you are going to a restaurant, you want to make sure that you are sticking to the vegetables, meats, and cheeses. It is best if you stick to the simplest meals as you can because most fast food places and restaurants are going to have a ton of extra carbs added to other ingredients.

Always avoid getting a bun. If you are going to a fast food place, you can simply tell them that you do not want the bun. You can also add other items such bacon it increases the fat you are getting.

If you decide to order a salad, make sure that you read the ingredients. What you will find is that many restaurants offer salads that are high in carbs.

If any of the food is breaded, just don't order it. Mozzarella sticks, chicken wings, or any other fried foods are usually breaded. If you do not have a choice, remove the breading before you eat the fried food.

It is also important that you be very careful when it comes to condiments. Dressings and sauces are a great way to add fat as well as flavor to your food but most of the time, you are going to find that they are packed full of sugar.

Be very careful when it comes to sauces that taste like sugar. Instead, try to used fattier dressings such as bleu cheese, ranch, or Caesar. If all else fails and you are at a sit-down restaurant, just as for a side of butter.

It is perfectly fine for you to ask for a special food when you are visiting a high-quality restaurant. Your waiter will know what is included in each food and you can ask for gluten-free versions or low carb.

If you are not sure about a specific food, just skip it. There are hidden carbs in all sorts of food and you do not want one meal to throw you out of ketosis. Don't risk it. Of course, if you know ahead of time you can look online and find out what foods are an option for you.

There are also apps that will allow you to input what you are eating and it will tell you how many carbs are in your food.

If you are in a hurry and need to stop at a fast food place, ordering a fatty bacon cheeseburger without a bun is a great option. Avoid the buns and the fries as well as the breaded chicken or anything smothered in barbeque sauce. Ketchup should be avoided as well.

The McDouble from McDonald's can be ordered without a bun, (you can ask them to replace it with lettuce) and without ketchup. It only contains 4g net carbs. If you keep the ketchup add an extra carb.

Ketogenic Eating on a Budget

There is no question that the Ketogenic diet is going to cost more than most diets. However, you have to ask yourself if you want to stuff your body with highly processed cheap food or do you want to provide your body with clean and healthy foods?

The first thing that you have to think about is the money that you are currently spending on foods such as cookies, chips, pasta, cakes, or rice. Since you are not going to be purchasing those any longer, you will start out saving a ton.

To goal of eating Ketogenic on a budget is to eat as healthy as you can while still spending as little as possible.

There are several techniques that you can use in order to purchase your food for a low price. You can use coupons, follow deals, buy the food in bulk, cook in bulk and freeze the meals, be mindful of what you are purchasing.

Using coupons to save money on all of the things that you buy will never get old. There are tons of different ways for you to get coupons. You can order them from clipping services online, get them out of the Sunday newspaper, print them or use coupon apps. Take advantage of those deals that are out there for you.

We all know that meat can get expensive. In fact, it is so expensive that it is usually the first thing that people cut out of their diet when they are trying to reduce their grocery bill. However, there are ways to save on meat. Did you know that when meat gets close to the expiration date, it is discounted at the grocery store?

You can purchase a ton of meat for a very low price and you don't have to worry about it going bad. When you purchase this discounted meat, you need to make sure that you are doing one of two things. One, cooking it as soon as you get it home. Or freezing it. Yep, you read that right; you can freeze the meat and then use it at your convenience without having to worry about it expiring.

Don't forget to watch for other store discounts and sales. Don't pass up those manager discount or buy 1 get 1 free offers. Top those sales with coupons and you are going to be saving a ton of money.

You shouldn't feel limited to purchasing all of your food at the grocery store. Instead, check out the prices online for items such as nuts, almond flour, or spices. What you will find is that they are about ½ of the price as they are at the grocery store. On top of that, if you take advantage of Amazon Prime, you will get free 2-day shipping!

Buy your foods in bulk, cook them in bulk, and then freeze them. I am not telling you to go and purchase a membership at Sam's club. There are so many other places that you can save money on your groceries. If you watch the sales flyers you will find that there are times when you should buy in bulk. Let me give you an example. This week at my local store, 5-pound bags of boneless skinless chicken breasts are on sale for 3 dollars per bag. Normally these are 8 dollars per bag and we use them a lot. I will be stocking up this week, getting as many as I can because it is not only going to save me money but it is going to ensure that I have the protein that we need.

What am I going to do with that chicken? Well, I'm going to put my Crock Pot to use of course. I will be making large batches of chicken that can be added to recipes, salads, or eaten as is. I will also be making a ton of meals in advance with the pre-cooked chicken which means that when it comes time to eat, all I have to do is heat the food up.

If you want to save money, it is very important for you to learn how to make food on your own. Okay, so you don't have to raise a cow but you should learn how to cook. (How great is it that you have a book packed full of Ketogenic recipes?)

The great thing about the recipes that you are going to find in the second half of this book is that they are not hard. They are cheap to make and you do not have to be a chef to make them. Making your food at home is going to ensure that you know exactly what is in your food and it is going to save you a ton of money.

You can even make your own dressings in about 15 minutes. The truth is, there isn't much that you can't make at home.

You will want to make sure that you have plenty of spices and seasonings in your cabinet. You can purchase containers of spices very cheap at stores like Aldi's or Save A Lot and don't worry just because the price is low, does not mean the quality is. Having plenty of spices on hand is going to ensure you can make a variety of meals.

You might find that you are having a hard time not drinking soda. Many people try to turn to diet soda, however, this is going to stop you from reaching the state of ketosis and it is going to cost you a lot of money. You may not realize it but drinking soda really does cost a lot. Instead, focus on drinking water, unsweetened teas, or coffee.

Coffee, tea, and water are great for you and they taste great as well. Since you can make so many different flavors, you are guaranteed to never get bored. On top of that, each different type of tea is going to provide you with different health benefits.

Brew a large amount of tea each time and just keep it with you. Or focus on drinking as much water as you can. You should make sure you are getting at least a gallon of water each day.

When it comes to purchasing vegetables, you want to purchase fresh if possible but you can also purchase frozen if your budget does not allow for fresh. The fresh vegetables are going to be a lot more expensive than the frozen versions however, they do contain the same vitamins. Try to eat spinach, cauliflower, and broccoli as they are going to provide you with the most nutrients. If you are making cauliflower rice, you will need fresh cauliflower which isn't the cheapest.

The best thing that you can do when it comes to saving money on the foods that you will need while following the Ketogenic diet is to shop around. You should not try to be loyal to one store or even 1 brand. Instead, focus on getting the best price. For example, I can regularly get my bacon for 1 dollar per pack because I am willing to go to a discount grocery store to purchase it. My vegetables? I go to Aldi of course. I don't think there is a cheaper place to get vegetables. I also purchase milk and eggs there. Right now, a gallon of milk is about 2 dollars and a dozen eggs are usually less than 30 cents.

It is also very important to make sure that the food that you purchase is going to work for you. For example, if you hate pork but find a great sale on pork, you need to ask yourself if you are actually going to be eating it. You see, if you get 20 pounds of pork for 20 dollars but you are not going to eat the pork, it is not going to save you any money.

Don't try to convince yourself that you will eat the food simply because it is cheap. What will most likely happen is that you will not eat the food and end up spending more money on food that you will actually eat.

Finally, there is cheese. Cheese is great to add fat to any recipe and it is delicious, however, it can be expensive as well. Did you know that when you purchase grated cheese it is coated with cornstarch to ensure that it does not stick together? It is also more expensive for you to purchase cheese that is already grated. Of course, there are going to be those times that you will be able to find it on sale.

However, you will have to decide if you want all of that cornstarch to be added to your diet. If you want to save money and make sure that you don't have the added carbs, purchase large blocks of cheese and toss them into your food processor to grate them right at home. 5 pounds of cheese will generally last a person on a Ketogenic diet about 2 weeks. As long as you eat the cheese within a few weeks, you do not have to worry about it going bad.

How To Stick With It

Before you jump right into the Ketogenic diet, you want to make sure that you start the right way. When you start the right way, you are going to avoid the mistakes that most people make while switching to the diet. This is also going to ensure that you begin seeing results and that you can enjoy the benefits of the Ketogenic diet much faster.

Because the Ketogenic diet is very low in carbohydrates, high in fat, and moderate when it comes to protein bone broth is a great thing to keep on hand. There are two recipes for bone broth at the end of this book. One of the recipes is for chicken and one is for beef. I would suggest that you always keep both of these bone broths on hand.

What a typical day would look like

When someone is following the Ketogenic diet they may eat bacon and eggs for breakfast, have a chicken salad for lunch with a cup of bone broth on the side and then have a nice steak with a side of sautéed vegetables for dinner. And of course a Ketogenic dessert later in the day.

As you can see this is not a restrictive diet at all. You are still going to be eating all three meals every day and you can even eat dessert every day. If you need a snack in between meals all you have to do is grab a handful of nuts instead of a piece of fruit.

One mistake that many people make when they begin the Ketogenic diet is that they do not get enough salt in their diet. This is not normally something that we think about because most diets consist of a lot of processed foods which already contain a lot of salt. However, when you are following the Ketogenic diet and you cut the processed foods out what you might find is that you become low on sodium.

Many people would not see this as a problem. How many times do we hear doctors telling people to cut down on the sodium or cut it out? However, when you are low on sodium you are going to feel fatigued and you are going to have a lot of cravings. Therefore it is important to ensure that you are getting enough.

Low potassium levels may also occur when you are following the Ketogenic diet. You will excrete more potassium when you follow the Ketogenic diet therefore it is important that you make sure you are replenishing it.

Most of us are already deficient in magnesium which is important to our sleep as well as our moods, muscles and overall well-being. Therefore it is very important that you are getting enough magnesium.

There is one thing that is going to provide you with all three of these... BONE BROTH. I cannot stress to you how important is that you make up several batches of bone broth and keep it on hand at all times.

When you start the Ketogenic diet it is vital that you stock up on those greens as well. Because the Ketogenic diet is low carb, many people just stop eating vegetables all together. Do not do this. Instead, eat vegetables that are green! Leafy green vegetables are going to provide you with tons of vitamins and minerals while keeping you fuller longer. Add them to your smoothies and salads or just sauté them!

Now onto sticking to it. If you have ever tried to make a change in your life or tried to start something new, then you know just how hard it can be. You see, we all start out strong. We want to make that change. We know the benefits of making the change and we know the change is good for us.

Then something happens. Something changes within us. We begin slipping back into our old habits. We lose the motivation that we had pertaining to whatever thing we were trying to change. This is why diets fail!

You see, it is very easy to forget that no matter what it is that we are learning, there are going to be some initial struggles. Do you remember how hard it was for you to learn how to drive? Eventually after a lot of practice, driving became second nature.

One of the great things about the Ketogenic diet is that a lot of the decision making that you would need to do with other diets is cut out. In the beginning, when you first start the diet, it is going to take a bit of work for you to stick to it however, eventually it is going to become second nature. Then all of that energy that you were wasting on decision making when it came to what you were going to eat can be used on something more important.

There are a few things that you can do which will help you stick to the Ketogenic diet. You want to make sure that you are sticking to it at least 90 percent of the time for the first 40 days because it is during this time that you will begin to form new habits. If you begin 'cheating' or eating foods that you know are not Ketogenic approved, you will make a habit of this and all of your work will be for nothing.

Therefore, in the first 40 days of following the Ketogenic diet, you want to make sure that 2 of your meals each day follow this rule: 70 percent of the calories will come from fat, 20 percent of the calories will come from protein, and 10 percent of the calories will come from carbohydrates.

If your brain becomes overwhelmed having to think about all of the fat, protein, and carbohydrates that are in each of your meals, you will not be able to stick to the plan. Therefore you want to make sure that you have 3 default meals. These are meals that you know you can eat, that follow the rule, and you don't have to think about them.

Of course, these meals do not have to follow the rule exactly, they can have more fat, as well as less carbs and protein however, they should never have more carbs or protein.

You want to pay attention to what happens when you do indulge and eat carbs. For example if you walk into your mom's house and the smell of fresh baked bread hits you, what you might find is that you are scarfing down bread before you realize what is going on.

It happens. We all have weaknesses. Over the next few days, I really want you to pay attention to how you feel. You're not going to have much energy and you won't be able to focus. This is going to remind you of why you began following the Ketogenic diet in the first place. You want more focus, more energy and more clarity.

If you find that you turn to food when you are stressed out, it is very important for you to understand what is causing you the stress and how you can deal with the stress, without turning to carbs. If you don't take the time to understand and learn how to handle the stress in the appropriate manner, you are not going to be able to stick to the changes that you will make when following the Ketogenic diet.

You need to be prepared for when hunger strikes. Have you ever been so busy that you just didn't take the time to eat? What happened when you finally decided it was time to get some food? Chances are that you probably grabbed whatever you could find and you didn't care if it was good for you or if it followed your diet. You just wanted his will happen when you are following the Ketogenic diet. Therefore it is important for you to be prepared.

Keep a Ketogenic snack at your desk so that you are not tempted to head off to the vending machine or kitchen. Have a plan as to what you are going to do on your breaks instead of grazing on processed junk. Know what you are going to make for dinner when you get home from work.

When you are prepared, you don't have to worry about what you will eat or making the right choices when you get hungry. You are already going to know what you are going to eat.

You also want to keep track of everything! How much water did you drink? How much did you exercise? How much fat did you eat? Protein? Carbs? Did you drink your bone broth today?

The truth is, it is just too much to remember it all. If you try to remember it all, you are just going to overload your brain and end up forgetting it anyway. This is going to result in failure. Instead, grab a planner and keep track of it all.

Chapter 2: What Is a Crock Pot

The Crock-Pot is actually one brand of the Crock Pot and over the years people have simply adapted that name for all Crock Pots, even though they come in many different brands.

The Crock-Pot actually paved the way for all Crock Pot brands when it was introduced in 1970. It was originally sold as a bean cooker. However, as time went on it was redesigned and eventually, it became the Crock Pot we use today.

Many different companies make the Crock-Pot style Crock Pot, and they can be found in almost every kitchen across the nation. We all love our Crock Pots.

You can make stews, soups, easy dinners, breakfasts, and even desserts in them. They are also great for making cheaper tough cuts of meat tender. On top of all of that, you can even use them to make your own bread (however, you will not be doing this).

As I said, over the years people have begun using the name brand, Crock-Pot, and Crock Pot interchangeably. That means that all of the recipes in this book can be cooked in any brand Crock Pot, not just the Crock-Pot brand.

The Crock Pot will use the moisture from the food that you are cooking and the heat to cook foods for a very long time. Often times this will be 4 hours, 6 hours, or 8 hours. The Crock Pot consists of three components that include a glass lid, a pot, and the heating element.

The Crock Pots ceramic pot will sit inside of the heating unit. Some of the Crock Pots will heat from the bottom, others will heat from the sides, and then there are those that will heat from both the bottom and sides. The pots come in many different sizes and are usually an oval or round.

The Crock Pots will only have two settings. You will have the low setting which you will use if you want to cook the food for 8 hours or more. This will bring the temperature up to about 200 degrees. Then you will have the high setting which you will use if you want to cook the food for 4 hours. This setting will bring the temperature up to about 300 degrees. There are some Crock Pots that come with a third setting and it is simply warm. You will choose this option if you want the food to stop cooking but want it to stay warm.

While the Crock Pot is on, it is going to continuously cook the food. There are, however, some models that will come with a timer, which will allow you to cook the food for a specific amount of time and then the cooker will shut off or switch to the keep warm setting.

There are some Crock Pots that actually sit on top of the heating unit instead of inside of it. Because the heat comes only from the bottom of the pot, the food may take longer to cook. If you have this type of Crock Pot, you will want to cook the recipes in this book for longer than what the recipe calls for. Using this type of Crock Pot also increases the chances of the food getting scorched on the bottom, therefore it is very important that you are able to stir the food often. Because the Crock Pot requires that you stir often, the lid must be removed. When the lid is removed, heat escapes which causes the cooking time to extend.

These types of Crock Pots tend to have more settings besides the low, high, and warm that we have already talked about. They also often power off and on during the cooking cycle instead of continuously cooking the food.

Why is there confusion?

The main reason that there is confusion between Crock-Pots and the Crock Pots is that Crock Pots are so much like the Crock-Pot brand. When a person thinks of a Crock Pot, they automatically think of the Crock-Pot style Crock Pot and they have just come to know all Crock Pots as Crock-Pots.

The good news is that it does not matter what brand of Crock Pot you own, it does not have to be a Crock-Pot brand. All of the recipes that are for Crock-Pots will work in a Crock Pot and all of the recipes for a Crock Pot will work in the Crock-Pot. All Crock Pots are going to cook the food slowly and on low heat.

About the Crock Pot
The Crock Pot is going to sit on the countertop and will be plugged into the wall via an A/C power cord. The lid is vented in order to release some of the steam as the temperature slowly increases as the food cooks.

The Crock Pot was designed so that food could cook unattended which allows us to add the ingredients in the morning and when we get home from work, enjoy dinner without having to stand over the stove for hours.

You will never need to preheat your Crock Pot and the foods that are cooked in the Crock Pot are going to retain their flavors because they are cooked in their own juices and they are cooked in a small space. As long as you do not remove the lid, the flavors are going to stay in the food instead of floating around the air in your home.

One great feature of the Crock Pot is that you can add frozen food to it. This means that if you forget to lay the food out the night before you plan on cooking it, you don't have to worry. Just toss it in the Crock Pot and let it cook.

If you want to reduce cleanup time, you can line the Crock Pot with foil or a Crock Pot liner. It is not advised for you to lift the lid and stir the food while it is cooking because this is only going to release the heat that has built up in the Crock Pot which means that it is going to take longer for the food to cook. However, you will find that some recipes call for you to stir the food during the last half hour of cooking.

What Can You Make in A Crock Pot?

There truly can be nothing more wonderful than walking into your home after a long day at work and smelling your favorite meal that has cooked all day just waiting for you. Of course, if you are using the Crock Pot while you are at home, smelling those delicious aromas can make you hungry but when the food is finally done at the end of the day, it is worth the wait.

So many of us are used to fast food when we are hungry or when we are so busy that we don't have time to stand over the stove and prepare a meal. We run to the closest fast food joint to grab a burger, however, while cooking in a Crock Pot is the complete opposite of fast food, it can be used in place of those types of foods if you do a bit of planning.

Believe it or not, the slow cooking method has been around since ancient times. Long ago, people learned that if they cooked meat or root vegetables at a low temperature for a long period of time, the food would become softer, tenderer, and therefore easier for them to eat.

The great thing about the Crock Pot is that there is virtually nothing that you cannot cook in it. You can make overnight oats for breakfast, burritos for lunch, lasagna, roast, or meatloaf for dinner, and even cake for dessert.

Coming home to a meal that is cooked to perfection is so much better than having to stop off at the drive-thru on the way home from work. Ask yourself, would you rather eat a home cooked meal or fast food? I will bet that you would rather sit down to a huge plate of home cooked food that is going to make you feel good and strong rather than some greasy burger that is going to make you sick later on.

While meat is often the most popular item to prepare in the Crock Pot, it is not the only type of food that you can make. If you are preparing meat, it is a good idea to thaw it because if you do not it is going to take longer for it to cook.

When you are cooking meat in the Crock Pot you need to make sure that the internal temperature of the meat reaches 140 degrees Fahrenheit very quickly so that the bacteria are not allowed to multiply. If you are cooking poultry in the Crock Pot it is a good idea to cook it with the skin on to ensure that it does not become dry.

Often times, the vegetables are going to take longer to cook than the meat. Therefore, it is a good idea to cut your vegetables into pieces that are all about the same size so that they all finish cooking at about the same time. You can also place the vegetables on the bottom of the Crock Pot and the meat on top to ensure that the vegetables get done cooking at about the same time as the meat.

Crock Pot Benefits

While the Crock Pot is not the best tool for every kitchen task, it does provide us with many benefits. Which include:

- Allowing food to cook for longer periods of time which helps to distribute flavors better.
- Cooking at a low temperature helps to reduce the chances of the food scorching, burning to the bottom of your pan, or getting burnt in the oven.
- The Crock Pot allows you to purchase less expensive cuts of meat or tougher cuts of meat because when the meat is cooked for a long period of time it becomes tender and tasty.
- The Crock Pot is going to free your oven up so that you can use it to make other dishes. This is great when it comes to the holidays or when you are going to have a large amount of people over.
- The Crock Pot also reduces the amount of time that you have to spend cleaning up. You don't have a ton of pots and pans to wash after dinner. Most of the time, you will only have to wash the Crock Pot.

- If you want to save money on your electric bill, the Crock Pot just might be the way to go. The Crock Pot uses much less energy than your electric oven is going to use.
- Many people only use their Crock Pot in the winter however, this should be reconsidered because unlike the oven the Crock Pot is not going to heat your house up when it is hot outside.
- When you are having a party at work or a potluck at a friend's house, make your dish in the Crock Pot because it travels well. All you have to do is pack up the entire Crock Pot and plug it in at your office or friend's house.
- One of the most popular reasons that people use the Crock Pot is for convenience. When you are cooking in the Crock Pot, you can leave your food unattended for the entire day and you don't have to worry about it burning. It is a great way to prepare a meal if you know that you are going to have a particularly busy day, if you are not feeling well or if you just don't feel like standing over the stove.
- If you are trying to lose weight, having your meal ready at home in your Crock Pot eliminates any temptation that you would have to order out or swing by the drive-thru. The meals that you cook in the Crock Pot are not only going to be delicious but nutritious as well.
- Crock Pots allow for easy meal preparation. Most of the time, all you have to do is place all of the ingredients in the Crock Pot and place the lid on it. The Crock Pot does the rest.
- Crock Pots are not only useful in the winter but they can be useful all year long. Most people love using their Crock Pot in the winter for soups and stews, however, they work just as well in the summer months.

Why use a Crock Pot?

If you are looking for a fun way to make lots of low cost and healthy meals for your family, the Crock Pot just might be the answer. Crock Pots do not cost a lot of money, unlike some of the newer cookers out there. They cost very little to operate and they can turn those inexpensive foods into something that your family loves.

Because the Crock Pot has been around for so long there are literally thousands of recipes that you can make in them. They are a great addition to any kitchen and are very easy to clean. But if you are still wondering why you should purchase and use a Crock Pot, here are a few reasons.

Crock Pots are frugal. Everyone is trying to save money right now and you can easily purchase a Crock Pot for about 30 dollars. This could actually save you hundreds of dollars when you compare it to purchasing all of the appliances that can do what the Crock Pot can. Not only is purchasing a Crock Pot going to save you money but what you will find is that over time, you will be able to reduce your grocery bill.

This very important when it comes to following the Ketogenic diet because buying high-end cuts of meat can be very expensive. However, when you use the Crock Pot, you can toss inexpensive cuts of meat in your soups or stews and they will still come out tasty and tender. When compared to using other appliances, the Crock Pot will save you money as well. I mentioned earlier in this book how the Crock Pot used less energy than the oven but did you know that you can use about 4000 watts of electricity when cooking with the oven and only 250 watts when using the Crock Pot?

The final frugal way that the Crock Pot can be used is by making use of all of those delicious leftovers. When you cook in the Crock Pot, it is likely that you are going to have some leftovers. These can be used for lunches or you can repurpose the leftovers and create a completely new meal for your family.

The Crock Pot can help you to improve your health. If you are like most people today, you rely a lot on fast food or prepackaged processed foods when it comes to mealtime. However, when you are using the Crock Pot to make your meals, you will be eliminating these prepackaged processed foods and fast foods from your diet. You will be replacing these foods with healthy delicious home-cooked meals.

Using the Crock Pot can result in you losing weight and feeling better than ever before because you are going to be eating whole natural foods. On top of this, if you have ever done any research about what is going into the processed foods that we are eating, then you will know that cooking your meals at home is going to ensure you know exactly what is going into your food and you are going to understand how important that is.

Imagine how great it will feel to serve your family a home cooked meal that is actually good for them even on your busiest of days. Imagine how great it is going to feel to sit down to a healthy delicious meal after a long day at work.

The Crock Pot makes cooking easy. You don't have to be a chef in order to use the Crock Pot. All you have to do is layer the food in the Crock Pot, place the lid on it, turn it on and walk away. It really is that easy. You can set your Crock Pot up in the morning before you head off to work and when you come home, dinner will be waiting on you. Most Crock Pot recipes are not that difficult to prepare and actually take no culinary skills.

It is very easy for you to clean your Crock Pot after you have served the meal. After dinner, all you have to do is place the leftovers in a container, and scrub that Crock Pot down. If you find that your foods are sticking to it, you can spray it with cooking spray before you place the food in it. After the Crock Pot has been washed all you have to do is place it back in the base and it is ready for the next meal to be prepared. Imagine, no more scrubbing pots and pans.

Meals that are prepared in the Crock Pot are delicious. One of the great things about the Crock Pot is that you really can't mess the recipes up. Everything that you toss into the Crock Pot is going to be amazing, even if it is just your own mixture of meat, vegetables, and spices. It always seems to turn out perfect. The vegetables and meat are always tender and they are infused with whatever herbs and spices you chose to use.

Of course, one of the biggest benefits to using the Crock Pot is that they are going to save you a ton of time. This is because you are able to cook your meals while you are at work or taking care of the kids. Talk about multitasking. In fact, as I am sitting here writing this right now, my dinner is simmering away in my Crock Pot. It feels so wonderful and is so freeing not to have to stand over the stove and babysit your food as it cooks. It is great to know that dinner is going to be perfect when it is done and to never have to worry about burning anything. You no longer have to waste your time worrying about the food burning but instead, you can go play with the kids, relax with your husband or spend some time working on your hobby.

The Crock Pot is one of the easiest methods of cooking, it is so easy for you to clean up after meal time, it saves you time as well as money and it can improve your health. What more could you want from one little appliance?

Crock Pot Tips and Tricks

If you have ever tossed a bunch of different ingredients into your Crock Pot in the morning and thought about how delicious your dinner was going to be all day long, only to come home to a pot of mush, you might feel like giving up. However, don't give up just yet. Here are the top tips and tricks that you can use to ensure you are the master of your Crock Pot in no time flat.

1. While you can use start with meat that is frozen, it is best to start with meat that it at room temperature. When it is possible you do not want to start with cold meat. The reason for this is because you really do want to brown the outside of the meat before you place it in the crock-pot. When you caramelize the outside of the meat, you are going to get a deep delicious flavor in your dish. I also suggest that when you do brown the meat, you do so only after you have seasoned it. This will create an amazing flavor.

2. Don't forget about the brown bits. The brown bits are the tiny morsels that are left in the pan after the meat has browned. They are packed full of flavor. You will want them in your Crock Pot. You can deglaze your pan by adding some stock, water, or even wine to the pan. Cook over medium heat while carefully scraping the browned bits off of the bottom of the pan with a wooden spoon. Most of these are going to dissolve into the liquid that you use which is going to make an amazing sauce.

3. If you do use wine in your Crock Pot, don't cook with any wine that you would not drink. Each of your ingredients should be quality ingredients. The Crock Pot is not a magic machine that is going to turn low-quality ingredients into high-quality food. Imagine how bad a cake would taste if you used old poor-quality chocolate.

4. If you add tomatoes to your recipes it is important to choose tomatoes that are not going to turn out mushy. Choose whole canned tomatoes instead of crushed. If you want the tomatoes to be in smaller pieces, simply chop them up before you put them in the in your Crock Pot. You can also use dried tomatoes but never do you want to use fresh tomatoes in your Crock Pot. They will simply turn into mush.

5. Don't freak out if you look into the Crock Pot and find that there is too much liquid. Simply transfer some of that liquid to a saucepan. You can make gravy out of it or use it to glaze the food.

6. If you open up your Crock Pot and find that your meat is perfectly cooked but your vegetables are overcooked, simply remove the vegetables that are overcooked. Never serve the dish with overcooked vegetables. Serve the meat with a side of freshly cooked vegetables. You can also puree the overcooked vegetables and mix them in with the sauce.

7. Make sure that you understand how your Crock Pot works. The high setting is used only when cooking foods for a shorter period of time. You do not want to leave your Crock Pot on the high setting for 10 or 12 hours because you are going to come back

to a burned mess. Make sure that you always check to ensure you are using the right setting.

8. You will find that some of the foods that you make in your Crock Pot are going to taste better the following day. This is because flavors have been able to develop as the food sits so many meat dishes and chilies are actually going to be better the day after you make them.

9. The great thing about Crock Pots is that the work very good with fattier cuts of meat. When you cook them on low and for a long period of time, the fat is going to ensure that the meat does not become dry. Since fattier cuts are generally the cheaper cuts this is actually a really great thing when it comes to your budget. Of course, this does not mean that you should not cook lean meats in your Crock Pot. It is fine for you to cook meats like chicken breast in the Crock Pot but it is best to do this on days when you know you are going to be around. I regularly cook several pounds of chicken breast in my Crock Pot and then shred it for the coming week. However, I do this on a day when I am home because it only takes a few hours on low heat for the chicken to cook. If I leave it in too long, I will not have delicious chicken but instead, I will have grossly dry chicken.

10. When you are using a Crock Pot, it is important to make sure that the food you add to it, is layered properly. Most of the time the source of heat will be at the bottom of the Crock Pot. This means that you need to place foods on the bottom of the Crock Pot that will take the longest to cook such as root vegetables, or tough cuts of meat. The more delicate vegetables should be at the top of the crock-pot or added within the last 30 minutes of cooking to ensure that they do not turn into mush.

11. Every time that you lift that lid will add about 30 minutes to the cook time so just don't do it. The Crock Pots come with a glass lid that allows you to see how the food is doing. So, do not open the Crock Pot until the end of the cooking time, then if you need to you can add other spices or ingredients.

12. Herbs and dairy should always be added at the end of the cooking process. You will only stir in items like sour cream right before you serve the dish. If you do this too early, the dairy product will curdle and ruin your entire dish.

13. Some of the vegetables that you add such as onions may add too much liquid to your recipe if you find that this is the case, simply remove the lid from the Crock

Pot for about 30 minutes and turn it on high. This is going to boil off the extra liquid.

14. Not all Crock Pots are the same so if while you are working through these recipes, you find that they are not cooking for the exact time that the recipe says they should it is okay. What that means is that your recipes may get done a bit sooner or a bit later than what the recipe says they will. This is simply because all Crock Pots are different. While mine may run a bit hot, yours may take a bit longer to heat up. If you notice that one recipe takes a bit longer to cook or that most of the recipes do, simply make a note of that and then you will know in the future that you will need to add a bit more time when cooking in the Crock Pot.

Safety and The Crock Pot

The Crock Pot was designed to cook foods for several hours and to heat the food to the proper temperatures, however, when it comes to food there are still a few precautions that you need to take.

The first thing that you need to do when it comes to safety is to make sure that you are never filling the pot more than ⅔ of the way full with food. It is also important for you to make sure that you do not take the lid off while the food is cooking in order to keep the safe temperature inside of the Crock Pot.

It is important that your Crock Pot heat your food to no less than 140 degrees within the first four hours of cooking to ensure that bacteria does not grow. For this reason, it is important for you to test the food and make sure that your Crock Pot is working properly.

You can test a Crock Pot by filling it ⅔ of the way full with water. Place the lid on the Crock Pot and turn it on to the low setting. Allow the water to cook for 8 hours. Using a food thermometer, check the temperature of the water. As long as the temperature is 185 or higher, the Crock Pot is working properly. On the other hand, if the temperature is less than 185 then the Crock Pot may not be functioning properly and it may not be safe to cook food in.

It is completely safe for you to leave the Crock Pot cooking while you are away from the house because they run off of such low wattage. Even though the base does heat up, the Crock Pot has been designed so that it does not get hot enough to set anything on fire.

When you are cleaning your Crock Pot, it is important that you never put the base of the Crock Pot in water. Most Crock Pots have a removable insert, however, if yours does not, simply wash the inside with a sponge and then wipe all of the spills away.

It is also important that you do not freeze the stoneware or try to use it on the stovetop because this can cause it to crack. Also putting the hot insert onto a countertop that is cold could cause it to crack as could filling it with cold water when it is still hot.

Even though the Crock Pot is designed to make sure that your food cooks completely and safely it is still important for you to check the internal temperatures of the food with a thermometer before you serve it.

When you need to add beans to a recipe it is very important that you do not use dry beans. When dry beans are cooked in a Crock Pot, they will release a toxin called Phytohemagglutinin. This can cause diarrhea, abdominal pain, vomiting, and nausea. Make sure that you soak the beans overnight or boil them in order to remove the toxin and ensure that the beans are safe to place in the Crock Pot. One way to make sure that the beans are safe is to soak them for no less than 12 hours and then rinse them. Boil the beans for 10 minutes before adding them to the Crock Pot. Of course, if you want to skip all of this, simply use canned beans.

The Crock Pot should only be used for cooking, not reheating. If you have leftovers, you can place them in the fridge within 2 hours after the meal. When you reheat, then you will want to do so in the microwave or on the stovetop and always make sure that the internal temperature is 165 degrees or higher.

Converting your Favorite Recipes into Crock Pot Recipes

Protein

The Crock Pot is one of the greatest pieces of equipment to have in your kitchen. It is great for making all sorts of recipes but what are you supposed to do when all of your family favorites have to be cooked on the stove top?

Are we just supposed to accept our fate of standing in front of the stove for hours on end in order to make our families happy? No! All you have to do is to convert those recipes over to Crock Pot recipes.

One of the strengths of the Crock Pot is how it is able to turn inexpensive tough cuts of meat into tender, juicy, tasty meals. However, as you have already learned, it is very easy for you to cook meats that are normally tender in the Crock Pot as well. You just have to keep an eye on them to make sure that they do not overcook. This does not mean that you have to watch them nonstop as they cook, there is quite a bit of room for error so do not be afraid to try this.

When using the Crock Pot, it is best to brown the outside of whatever meat you are cooking unless you want to be able to shred it. Not only is browning the meat going to help to keep it together but it is going to seal the flavor in as well.

If you are using hamburger or sausage in your Crock Pot, you will want to make sure that it is fully cooked and drained before it is put in the Crock Pot. If you do not cook the meat before putting it in the Crock Pot, it is going to turn to mush and be a gross color. If a meat comes fully cooked, such as some sausage, you should slice them and brown them. This also applies to tofu.

You will quickly sear seafood but make sure that you do not overcook it. This will only be added to the Crock Pot during the last 30 minutes of cooking.

Vegetables

One of the most important things that you have to think about when you are converting any recipe to a Crock Pot recipe is the vegetables that you will be putting in it. Are the vegetables hardy? How are the vegetables cooked in the original recipe? Are they simply softened or are they roasted? How does the size of the vegetables compare to the size of the meat?

The first rule when it comes to vegetables and your Crock Pot is that all of the vegetables that will be going in at the same time should be close to the same size. It does not matter if the recipe calls for you to cut one vegetable smaller than the other, they should be the same size so they cook for the same amount of time.

Vegetables such as onions should not be put in raw unless you like a very strong flavor. Some people recommend browning the onions and even garlic first. Personally, I love to add raw onion to my recipes because I love the flavor. If you brown the onions it is best to add them halfway through the cooking process because they can disintegrate during the cooking process.

Vegetables that are not quick cooking but are not as hardy as potatoes will go in the Crock Pot halfway through the cooking process. These would be vegetables such as cauliflower or broccoli. The quick cooking vegetables like corn or peas will go in about 30 minutes before the meal is done.

I suggest that you not use frozen vegetables in your Crock Pot if at all possible because they are going to reduce the temperature of the liquid when you add them and this could cause bacteria to grow. It is fine to heat them on the stovetop before adding them but you don't want to just defrost them because they will end up being soggy.

Liquid

When you are cooking food in a Crock Pot, you will need some type of liquid. The food is cooked in the liquid. It is important that you add between 1 and 2 cups of liquid at the beginning of the cooking process. You can add more later as long as you have brought it to a boil if you need to. If you find that there is too much liquid, simply drain it or allow it to steam off.

You really only want enough water to cover the food that is being cooked. Since you will be cooking with the lid on the Crock Pot, the liquid will not reduce very much. However, you do need to remember if the liquid gets to the point that it is not covering the food, you will want to add more. It must be boiling so that you do not lower the temperature inside of the pot.

If your recipe calls for a slurry to thicken it, you will never start with that. Instead, you will cook the recipe without using the slurry then about 30 minutes before serving you will make the slurry using the liquid out of the Crock Pot and cornstarch or flour. Then add the slurry into the Crock Pot, whisking to get rid of any clumps. Allow this to cook for about 30 minutes or until thickened.

Seasonings

If you are using seasonings that are not strong in flavor you can add them when you first begin however, you will want to reduce the amount by about half. Remember if this is not enough, you can always add more later.

If you are using strong spices or delicate spices you will want to add them about a half of an hour before you serve the dish. You can also add more of the spices you added earlier if needed.

If the recipe requires wine it is best to reduce the wine on the stovetop before adding it to the Crock Pot. Most of the time when alcohol is added to a recipe the alcohol will cook off and leave great flavors. However, because the Crock Pot cooks with the lid on the entire time, this is not going to happen. If you do not want to reduce the wine before adding it to the Crock Pot, you can remove the lid from the Crock Pot at the end of the cooking process and allow it to cook for 30 more minutes.

Salt should not be added early on in the cooking process especially if you are using stocks or broths that you have purchased at the store. The salty flavor will intensify most of the time and because you can't taste the raw meat you will not know if you have added too much salt. Instead, add the salt 30 minutes before serving the dish.

Cooking Times

Of course, it is going to take the Crock Pot long to cook the dishes that you convert to Crock Pot recipes. There is no definite way to convert the time because some dishes are just going to take longer than others. However, if you follow the formula below, you will be fairly close to the proper cooking time for all of your dishes. Remember it is important for you to keep the lid on the Crock Pot the entire time that you are cooking because if you remove it during the cooking process, it is only going to take long for the food to cook.

It is okay for you to check the food at the halfway mark and the half-hour mark, however, you shouldn't worry about checking it more often than that, no matter how tempting it may be.

Oven/ Stovetop Time	Crock Pot Setting and Time
15-30 minutes	Low for 4 to 6 hours
31-40 minutes	Low for 6 to 8 hours or high for 3-4 hours
41 minutes - 3 hours	Low 8 to 10 hours or high for 4 to 6 hours

If you follow these guidelines, you will be able to convert any recipe to a Crock Pot recipe which means that you are not going to be spending hours standing in front of your stove when you could be doing other stuff that you actually enjoy. This is also going to allow you to make all of your favorite dishes for your family even when you don't have a lot of time to cook.

Converting your recipes to a Crock Pot recipe is very easy. It is also very important for you to be able to do. While all of the recipes in the next chapter are for a Crock Pot, you will find that a couple of them have alternative directions which you can follow to cook them on the stove top or in the oven.

However, learning how to convert recipes to Crock Pot recipes is very important because it allows us to take our favorite recipes and make them in the Crock Pot. When we do this, we are able to have all of our favorite foods waiting for us when we get home from work instead of standing over the hot stove for hours after a long day at work.

When you are converting your recipes to Crock Pot recipes, there are a few things that you need to know. The first is how long you will be cooking your foods in your Crock Pot versus when you cook them in the oven. We covered this at the end of the last chapter. However, I do suggest that if you are converting a new recipe to your Crock Pot, or trying a new recipe out, you will want to do so on a day when you will be able to be near the Crock Pot.

You see, Crock Pots are going to vary depending on make, model, style, and age. This means that it might take your Crock Pot much less time than it would take my Crock Pot to cook the exact same foods.

One of the great things about cooking in a Crock Pot is that you can make your meals ahead of time. This is called making freezer meals. When you make freezer meals, instead of prepping just one of a specific meal, you will prep 4. Three of these will go into your freezer bags while one will go into your Crock Pot.

Some people even go as far as making a month's worth of meals at the same time. This can take about 4 hours but it is a great way to ensure that you stay on track when it comes to the ketosis diet. It is also a great way to ensure that you have healthy meals ready and waiting for you even when you are tired so that you don't become tempted by highly processed junk that will stop you from reaching the state of ketosis.

If you are trying to follow the Ketogenic diet while sticking to a budget, the freezer meal technique is a great way to save money. You are going to be making your meals in bulk and you can actually make meals for a family of 4 for about 3 to 6 dollars per meal.

After the meals are frozen, all you have to do is pull them out of the freezer, the night before you plan you plan on eating them. In the morning when they have thawed, you will toss them into your Crock Pot and cook them according to the recipe.

Crock Pot Hacks

Did you know that it is not always necessary for you to add liquid to your Crock Pot when you are cooking meats? For example when you cook a whole chicken you never want to add any water or liquid otherwise you will end up with nothing more than a boiled chicken. The same is true when it comes to boneless skinless chicken breast or other meats that you want to cook alone for shredding.

If you want to cook your boneless skinless chicken breast in your Crock Pot for shredding to using in foods such as salads, or to use as a snack, all you need to do is toss the chicken breast (frozen or thawed) into the Crock Pot with whatever seasoning you want to use. Place the lid on top and then let it cook on low heat for 4 hours. Once the chicken is done cooking, you will strain the liquid off of it, rinse off any of the white slimy bits and then shred it.

Many people feel that the Crock Pot is a hassle because they have to do the prep work in the morning when they are already in a rush. However, if you know that you are going to be busy in the morning hours, you can prep the food the night before.

You can place the prepped food in the Crock Pot dish. Make sure that you cover the dish and place it in the fridge. When you get up the next morning, remove the dish from the fridge and then place it in the Crock Pot. Let this sit for 20 minutes before turning the Crock Pot on so that you do not raise the temperature of the dish too quickly causing it to crack.

When you are using the Crock Pot, it is best for you to use the low setting whenever possible. Of course there are going to be times when you are going to want to increase the temperature to the high setting however, cooking on low ensures that all of the flavors of the food are brought out. It also ensures that the food does not burn if you are away for a bit longer than expected.

You can actually cook two dishes at the same time in your Crock Pot by creating a foil wall to place in the middle of the Crock Pot. Place your Crock Pot liner in the Crock Pot over the foil wall and cook both dishes at the same time. This is a great way for you to cook a meat dish and a side dish or a dessert at the same time.

It is important when you are using your Crock Pot that you remember to always add the dairy near the end of the cook cycle. If you add the dairy products too early in the cook cycle it will curdle and ruin your meal.

Using the Crock Pot makes meal prep very easy but then there's that pesky Crock Pot that needs to be cleaned. In order to eliminate the clean up, use a liner in your Crock Pot. Then when you are done eating your meal, all you have to do is pull out the liner, throw it away, give the Crock Pot a quick wipe down and then it is ready for you to prepare your next meal.

When you are cooking foods such as fish, baked goods or other delicate items that are hard to remove from the Crock Pot, use a cooker sling. All you have to do is to line the Crock Pot with foil or parchment paper. When you are ready to remove the food from the Crock Pot, all you have to do is slide the sling out. Of course, this is going to make cleanup a breeze.

If you have avoided using the Crock Pot because you hate cleaning up the tough residue, you can let the Crock Pot clean itself! All you have to do is to fill the Crock Pot up with water to just above the residue. Add in ½ of a cup of baking soda as well as ½ of a cup of white distilled vinegar. Place the lid on the Crock Pot and set the heat to low. Allow this mixture to work for 1 to 4 hours. After 4 hours, allow the Crock Pot to cool. Rinse with warm water. Your insert will be spotless! (you can also use this mixture in your pans that you use on your stovetop if you burn food to them. Just bring them to a boil and then let them cool.).

In order to prevent needing to scrub your Crock Pot, coat the inside of it with coconut oil before you place your food in it. Of course if you are making soups and stews you do not have to do this because there is so much liquid that the food will not stick. However, when you are making meat dishes or those that tend to stick to the sides, the coconut oil will prevent sticking.

It is also a good idea to preheat your Crock Pot when you need to add foods to it that have been browned, seared, or sautéed before adding them to the Crock Pot. All you have to do is to turn the Crock Pot on high heat in order to bring it up to temperature quickly. This will help to ensure you are not adding cooking time on when you place hot food in a cold Crock Pot.

When you are cooking foods that are going to take up less space such as chicken breasts, place aluminum foil over the top of the Crock Pot before placing the lid on it in order to seal the moisture in.

One of the great benefits of using the Crock Pot is that you can use it to keep any food warm. Not ready to eat when the food is ready? All you have to do is to switch it over to the warm setting and let the Crock Pot keep the food warm while you get ready to eat. What is even better is that you don't have to worry about the food burning.

The Crock Pot is an amazing too and trust me, once you start using it on a regular basis, you are going to find yourself wondering how you ever lived without it. The truth is, about 90 percent of my meals are cooked in the Crock Pot. It is so versatile, you can cook almost anything in it, you never have to worry if you forgot to thaw your food out, and it is almost impossible to mess the food up when you are suing the Crock Pot.

The Crock Pot is so great at making sure that your food tastes amazing that it almost does not matter what you toss into it. The Crock Pot is great for using up all of those leftover ends and bits without creating a mess of a meal that you cannot eat.

It can cook your breakfast, lunch, dinner, snacks, and desserts. The Crock Pot is such a huge kitchen helper that many people are actually purchasing two or three of them so that they are able to cook all of their meals in them. Imagine having one Crock Pot to cook your breakfast in while you are sleeping. Another to have your dinner prepped in overnight so you can cook it as soon as you wake up in the morning. And finally another Crock Pot for those delicious Ketogenic desserts that you are going to want to enjoy every single night!

Of course, if you are just starting out using the Crock Pot, you may not be ready to use more than one at a time. It is best if you start with one Crock Pot and learn how to use it before adding in other Crock Pots but no matter how many Crock Pots you want to use, the Crock Pot is sure to make your life much easier. It is also guaranteed to help you to stick with the Ketogenic diet because you are not going to be tempted to grab some unhealthy processed food that will force you out of the state of ketosis. Instead, you will have healthy meals right at the tip of your fingers ready to eat that are going to help you focus better, have more energy, and to think more clearly.

Chapter 3: 5 Ingredient Ketogenic Crock Pot Recipes

Breakfast Recipes

Breakfast Casserole

Serves: 4

Ingredients

- 2 tbsp coconut oil
- 8 eggs
- 1 ½ cups sausage
- 1 cup chopped kale
- 2 tsp minced garlic

Method

1. Coat the bottom and sides of the Crock Pot with coconut oil.
2. Beat the eggs in a large bowl, then add in the minced garlic.
3. Pour the eggs into the Crock Pot and sprinkle the kale throughout the eggs. Top with the sausage.
4. Place the lid on the Crock Pot and turn the setting to low. Cook for 2 hours on the low setting then serve.

Egg and Spinach Casserole

Serves: 4

Ingredients

- 6 eggs
- 10 ounces of frozen spinach that has been thawed and drained
- 16 ounces of small curd cottage cheese
- 16 ounces of shredded cheddar
- ½ cup melted butter

Method

1. Beat the eggs together in a bowl.
2. Mix in the cottage cheese, cheddar, spinach, and the butter.
3. Pour the mixture into the bottom of a well-greased Crock Pot and then place the lid on the Crock Pot.
4. Cook over low heat for 2 hours.

Mexican Spinach Casserole

Serves: 4
Ingredients

- 2 lbs ground pork
- 2 cans of Rotel tomatoes drained
- 8 ounces of mozzarella cheese shredded
- 16 ounces of cream cheese
- 20 ounces of frozen spinach, thawed and drained
- 4 tsp taco seasoning

Method

1. Brown the ground pork.
2. Once the pork is brown, add the taco seasoning and then transfer the pork to the Crock Pot.
3. Add in the Rotel, as well as the cream cheese and mozzarella. Mix well.
4. Place the lid on the Crock Pot and cook on low heat for 1 hour.

Mushroom, Mozzarella, Feta, and Kale Casserole

Serves: 6

Ingredients

- 12 ounces of white mushrooms
- 8 ounces of kale that has been chopped finely
- 5 ounces of Feta, crumbled
- ¾ cup mozzarella cheese, shredded
- 12 eggs

Method

1. Beat the eggs until they are completely combined.
2. Sprinkle in the rest of the ingredients and mix well.
3. Spray your Crock Pot with nonstick cooking spray to ensure that the mixture does not stick as it is cooking.
4. Pour the mixture into the Crock Pot and place the lid on the Crock Pot.
5. Choose the low setting and cook for 2 hours.

Ham and Cheese Pocket

Serves: 1

Ingredients

- ¾ cup mozzarella cheese, shredded
- 1 ounce of cream cheese
- 4 tbsp of flaxseed meal
- 3 ounces of ham
- 3 ounces of provolone cheese (or any cheese that you like) sliced

Method

1. Begin by preparing the dough. Place the shredded mozzarella cheese and the cream cheese in a microwave-safe bowl and microwave for 1 minute.
2. After 1 minute, add in the flaxseed meal and stir until the dough is created.
3. Roll the dough out and then add the ham and the sliced cheese on one side of the rolled out dough. Fold the dough over and seal it.
4. Use a fork to poke a few holes in the pocket and then place in the Crock Pot for 1 hour on high heat.
5. When the pocket is done, allow it to rest for about two minutes and then cut it in half. Serve while it is still hot.

Bacon, Avocado, Eggs

Serves: 1

Ingredients

- 4 strips of bacon, uncured
- 1 avocado, sliced
- 2 eggs
- ¼ tsp salt

Method

1. Place the eggs in your Crock Pot and blend them well.
2. Chop the strips of bacon and add them as well as the avocado to the Crock Pot.
3. Sprinkle the salt.
4. Place the lid on the Crock Pot and cook on low heat for 2 hours.

Basic Breakfast Omelet

Serves: 1
Ingredients

- 2 eggs
- ¼ onion, diced
- A handful of kale or spinach
- ½ avocado, sliced
- Salsa
- 1 tsp coconut oil

Method

1. Beat the eggs together in a small bowl.
2. Mix in the greens and the onion with the eggs.
3. Pour coconut oil into your Crock Pot at high heat.
4. Once the coconut oil has melted, pour the egg mixture and reduce the heat to medium.
5. After 15 minutes, add in the avocado and salsa, then allow it to cook for another 45 minutes.
6. Serve and enjoy

Granola

Serves: 4
Ingredients

- 5 tbsp ground flaxseed meal
- 5 tbsp coconut flakes, unsweetened
- 1 tbsp chia seeds
- 1.5 ounces of Ketogenic approved nuts
- 4 tbsp sugar-free maple syrup

Method

1. Place all of the ingredients in a bowl and mix well.
2. Place the mixture in your Crock Pot and allow it to cook on low heat for 4 hours.
3. Once the mixture has cooked, place it on a cookie sheet and allow it to cool.

Crème Brûlée

Serves: 4

Ingredients

- 2 cups heavy cream
- 6 egg yolks
- ¼ tsp vanilla bean powder

Method

1. Place all of the eggs, heavy cream and vanilla powder in a medium bowl.
2. Beat this mixture until it is completely smooth.
3. Place the mixture into 4 ramekins, then place it into the Crock Pot.
4. Fill the Crock Pot with water until the ramekins are halfway submerged.
5. Cook on low heat for 4 hours.

Ketogenic Meats

Beef

Taco Casserole

Serves: 4

Ingredients

- 2 lbs ground beef
- 2 diced onions
- 2 (15 ounce cans) of diced tomatoes
- A packet of taco seasoning

Method

1. Brown the beef in a skillet and then add the diced onions and cook for 5 minutes.
2. Place the beef, diced onions, and tomatoes into the Crock Pot, then add the taco seasoning and mix well.
3. Cook on low heat for 6 hours.
4. Sprinkle the cheese on top and enjoy.

Shepard's Pie the Ketogenic Way

Serves: 4

Ingredients

- 2 lbs ground beef
- 3 diced onions
- 3 heads of cauliflower
- 2 tbsp of your favorite spices (chili powder, cumin, Italian seasoning, onion powder, or garlic powder, etc.)

Method

1. Brown the ground beef in a large skillet over medium heat.
2. After the meat is browned, drain off about ½ of a cup of the oil and save it for later. Leave any remaining oil in the pan.
3. Place the onions in the skillet with the ground beef and cook for another 3 minutes over medium heat or until the onions are soft.
4. Place the cauliflower in a food processor until it is smooth. This will take about 5 minutes. Do this until you have pureed all of the cauliflower.
5. Place the cauliflower in a large bowl and then season it with the oil from the meat.
6. Add your spices to your beef and mix well.
7. Place the beef mixture in a your Crock Pot and then spread the cauliflower on top of the meat in an even layer.
8. Place the lid on the Crock Pot and cook on low for 6 hours.

Green Beef Scrambled

Serves: 4

Ingredients

- 1 lb ground beef
- 1 diced onion
- 6 cups diced spinach
- 4 eggs
- Salt and pepper

Method

1. Break up the ground beef into little pieces as you add it to your Crock Pot.
2. Add in the diced onion. Stir well.
3. Season the mixture with salt and pepper.
4. Place the lid on the Crock Pot and cook for 2 hours on medium heat.
5. After the beef has cooked for 2 hours, remove the lid then add in the spinach.
6. Allow this to cook for about 5 more minutes with the lid on or until the spinach is wilted.
7. While the spinach cooks, place the eggs in a bowl and season them with salt and pepper. Mix well.
8. Pour the eggs into the beef mixture and stir well.
9. Cook for an additional 20 minutes. Stir well and serve.

Beef, Onion, and Tomato Soup

Serves: 4

Ingredients

- 2 lbs ground beef
- 4 onions, sliced
- 2 (12 ounce) cans of tomato sauce

Method

1. Place the ground beef in a skillet over medium heat. Break the beef up using your spoon.
2. Once the beef is done browning, add in the sliced onions. Allow the onions to cook for about 5 minutes.
3. After the onions have cooked, place it with all of the ingredients into your Crock Pot.
4. Place the lid on the Crock Pot and cook on low heat for 6 to 8 hours.

Beef Bone Broth

While this is not a meal, it can be used as a snack or to make other meals with. It is also a great way for you to use up the extra bits of beef and ensure that you are getting enough collagen in your diet.

Ingredients

- 1 ½ to 2 lbs of beef bones (You can purchase these very cheap at the farmers market. You can also add in any extra fat that you have from previous beef purchases.)
- 1 tbsp white distilled vinegar
- 12 cups water (depending on the size of your Crock Pot)
- Chopped onions (optional if you want to add extra flavor)

Method

1. Place the bones and fat into your Crock Pot and fill the Crock Pot with water. The more water that you add to the Crock Pot, the more broth you are going to get so make sure you add as much as possible.
2. Add in vegetables (optional), and then add in the vinegar. At this point, you can also add salt or any other seasoning that you want to use.
3. Turn the Crock Pot on low heat and place the lid on the Crock Pot.
4. Allow the broth to cook for 12 hours. The longer that you cook the broth, the better it is going to be.
5. After the broth has cooked, use a cheesecloth to strain it. This is going to catch all of the extra bits of fat, meat, and bone.
6. Place the broth in a container and place the container in the fridge for at least 8 hours.
7. This is going to allow the fat to solidify at the top of the container. Once the fat has solidified, scrape it off of the broth.

You can use this for cooking or drink it as a snack. This makes a huge amount of servings however, the number will depend on the size of your Crock Pot.

Beef, Cabbage and Vegetable Stir Fry in the Crock Pot

Serves: 4

Ingredients

- 2 lbs ground beef
- 1 head of cabbage, shredded
- 2 onions, diced
- 3 cups celery, diced
- You can also add in soy sauce alternative or salt and pepper if desired

Method

1. Break the ground beef up into small bits into the Crock Pot, then add in the onions. Stir Well.
2. Add in the chopped celery and soy sauce. If you are using salt and pepper you can add it at this point.
3. Place the lid on the Crock Pot and cook over low heat for 6 hours.
4. Once the mixture has cooked for 6 hours, add in the shredded cabbage. Stir well, place the lid back on the Crock Pot and cook another 60 minutes.
5. Season with salt and pepper and then stir well.
6. Serve hot.

Green Chili Beef

Serves: 4
Ingredients
- 1 lb ground beef
- 1 onion, diced
- 12 ounces of diced green chilies
- 1 head of cauliflower, cut into florets
- 4 eggs, whisked together

Optional:
- ½ tsp garlic powder
- Salt and pepper
- Green onions, diced

Method
1. Into the Crock Pot, add in the beef and the green chilies and mix everything together.
2. Place the cauliflower in your food processor and puree it until it becomes cauliflower rice. Place the cauliflower rice in the Crock Pot with the beef mixture.
3. Add in the garlic powder if you are using it as well as the salt and pepper. Add the whisked eggs to the cauliflower rice mixture. Mix well.
4. Cook everything in the Crock Pot on medium heat for 5 hours.
5. If you are using the diced green onions, you will sprinkle these on the top before serving.
6. Enjoy

Pepper Encrusted Pot Roast

Ingredients
- A large pot roast that will fit into your Crock Pot
- Salt
- Pepper
- A sprig of rosemary

Method
1. Pat your roast dry using a paper towel.
2. Coat the outside of the roast with the salt and the pepper making sure that you press the salt and pepper firmly into the roast.
3. Place the roast into the Crock Pot and add the rosemary.
4. Place the lid on the Crock Pot and turn the heat to the low setting. Cook the roast for no less than 8 hours.
5.

The longer that you let the roast cook, the more tender it is going to be. You can add vegetables to this if you want, however, if you are going to cook this roast for a long time it is better to add the vegetables later on in the cooking process so that they do not become mushy.

Corned Beef Hash

Serves: 4

Ingredients

- 2 cups corned beef, chopped
- 1 onion, chopped
- 1 lb radishes, trimmed and quartered
- 2 garlic cloves, minced
- ½ cup beef broth
- Salt and pepper

Method

1. Add all the vegetables in your Crock Pot along with the corned beef. Mix well
2. Add in the beef broth and place the lid on the Crock Pot.
3. Allow this to cook for about 6 hours on low heat.
4. The liquid should reduce. Stir the mixture and season with salt and pepper if desired.

Green Curry Beef

Ingredients
- 1 onion, cut into chunks
- 2 lbs beef stew meat
- 1 can of coconut milk
- 3 tbsp Green Curry Paste

Method
1. Toss the beef stew meat and the onions into the bottom of the Crock Pot.
2. Add in the rest of the ingredients and mix well.
3. Place the lid on the Crock Pot and set the heat on the low setting.
4. Allow the mixture to cook for 8 hours. Serve hot.

Greek Meatballs

Serves: 4

Ingredients

- 1 ½ lbs ground beef
- ¼ cup of fresh basil, chopped
- ¼ cup of sun-dried tomatoes, chopped
- 1 tbsp garlic salt
- 2 eggs
- A pinch of pepper if desired

Method

1. Place all of the ingredients into a large bowl and mix well using your hands.
2. After everything is mixed, begin forming balls and setting them on a plate.
3. Once the balls are formed, place them into the Crock Pot and cook them on low heat for 6 hours.

Pumpkin and Beef Stew

Serves: 4 to 6

Ingredients

- 0.7 lb of beef stew meat
- 0.4 lb of chopped pumpkin
- 6 tbsp coconut oil
- 1 tbsp your favorite mixed herbs
- Salt and pepper

Method

1. Place the beef stew meat in your Crock Pot with ½ of your coconut oil.
2. Season with salt and pepper.
3. Cook this on high heat for 1 hour.
4. Once the beef stew meat has cooked for 1 hour, add the mixed herbs and the chopped pumpkin.
5. Top with the rest of your coconut oil.
6. Place the lid on the Crock Pot and cook on low heat for 4 more hours.
7. Stir well before serving.

Cabbage Rolls

Serves: 4 to 6

Ingredients

- 1 lb ground beef
- 1 cup parmesan
- 1 cup no sugar marinara sauce
- 1 tsp onion powder
- 12 cabbage leaves

Method

1. Blanch the cabbage until they are just tender enough to bend.
2. While the cabbage is cooking, place ½ of a cup of marinara sauce into the bottom of your Crock Pot.
3. Mix the meat, parmesan, and onion powder together in a bowl as well.
4. Once the cabbage is ready, allow it to cool so that you can handle it.
5. Place ¼ of a cup of the meat mixture into each cabbage leaf and then roll it up.
6. Place the rolled up cabbage into the Crock Pot with the seam down.
7. Pour the remaining marinara sauce over the cabbage rolls and then place the lid on your Crock Pot.
8. Cook the cabbage rolls on low heat for 8 to 10 hours or on high heat for 5 hours.

Italian Beef

Serves: 4

Ingredients

- 1 lb ground beef
- 1 jar of your favorite spaghetti sauce
- Bell peppers, 1 yellow, 1 red, and 1 green, chopped
- 8 ounces of mushrooms, chopped
- 4 handfuls of spinach

Method

1. Place all the ingredients except the spinach into the Crock Pot. Mix well.
2. Cook on low heat for 6 hours.
3. Once the beef has cooked for 6 hours, add in the spinach and allow it to cook until it wilts or for about 15 minutes.
4. This is a great dish served over rice.

Stuffed Bell Peppers

Serves: 3

Ingredients

- 6 bell peppers
- 1 onion, chopped
- 1 ½ lbs ground beef
- Salt and pepper

Method

1. Place the onions in a skillet and caramelize them.
2. Add in the ground beef and brown it.
3. Season with salt and pepper.
4. While the ground beef is cooking, cut the tops off of all of the bell peppers and remove the seeds from the inside.
5. Place the bell peppers in a large pot of boiling water and boil them for about 5 minutes.
6. After the bell peppers are done boiling, remove them from the water and turn them upside down to ensure there is no water in them.
7. Fill the bell peppers with the beef mixture. You can also top these with mozzarella cheese.
8. Place the bell peppers into the Crock Pot and allow them to cook on low heat for 4 to 6 hours.

Spicy Beef

Serves: 4 to 6

Ingredients

- 1 tri-tip roast
- 1 onion, chopped
- 2 cans of fire roasted tomatoes
- A few of your favorite hot peppers if you want it extra spicy

Method

1. Place all of the ingredients in the Crock Pot.
2. Cook for 8 hours on low heat.

** This is great served in lettuce wraps or over rice.

Poultry

Roasted Chicken

Serves: 4 to 6, depending on the size of the chicken

Ingredients

- 1 whole chicken
- 2 tbsp paprika powder
- 2 tbsp salt
- 2 tbsp black pepper
- 2 tbsp garlic powder

Method

1. Rinse your defrosted chicken in cool water. Make sure that you pull out the giblets (you can save these for later if you would like as they are packed full of nutrients).
2. Place the paprika powder, salt, pepper, and garlic powder in a small bowl. Mix well.
3. Rub the spice mixture over the entire chicken.
4. Before placing the chicken in a Crock Pot, take four balls of aluminum foil (to hold the chicken off of the bottom of the Crock Pot) and place them in the bottom of the Crock Pot.
5. Place the prepared chicken in the Crock Pot and cook on low for 6 to 8 hours.

Indian Drumsticks

Serves: 4 to 6

Ingredients

- 10 drumsticks
- 3 tbsp salt
- 4 tbsp garam masala
- ½ tbsp coconut oil

Method

1. Use the coconut oil to grease your Crock Pot.
2. Place the garam masala and the salt in a bowl. Mix well.
3. Use a paper towel to dry off the drumsticks.
4. Coat the drumsticks with the garam masala mixture and then place them in the Crock Pot. You want to make sure that none of the drumsticks touch each other.
5. Cook on low heat for 8 hours.

Roasted Whole Chicken In the Crock Pot

Serves: 3 to 5, depending on the size of the chicken

Ingredients

- One whole chicken (between 3 and 5 lbs)
- Olive oil
- Garlic powder
- Paprika powder
- Rosemary

Method

1. Remove the chicken from the package and pull out the innards.
2. Rinse the chicken off and pat it dry using a paper towel.
3. Place your chicken in your Crock Pot with the breasts down.
4. Drizzle it with a bit of olive oil, and add the spices.
   (Do not add any liquid to the Crock Pot. The chicken is going to produce enough liquid for it to cook. If you add liquid, you are not going to have a roasted chicken but instead, you will have a boiled chicken!)
5. Place the lid on your Crock Pot and turn the setting to low heat.
6. Cook the chicken for 6 hours.
7. Once the chicken is done it will easily pull from the bone.

If you do cook the chicken for more than 6 hours, it is going to first fall apart and then it will begin to burn.

Remember don't toss out those bones! Instead, throw them in the Crock Pot and make some chicken broth while you are sleeping.

Chicken Broth

Ingredients

- Save the chicken carcass and skin from the last recipe
- 5 stalks of celery
- 1 quartered onion
- Water
- Salt and pepper to taste

Method

1. Toss all of the ingredients into your Crock Pot.
2. Fill the Crock Pot with water making sure that you leave about 1 inch of space at the top.
3. Place the lid on the Crock Pot and select the high setting.
4. Cook for 8 hours or overnight.
5. After the mixture has cooked overnight, use a slotted spoon to remove all of the large ingredients.
6. Place a cheesecloth over a bowl and pour the mixture over it. This is going to get out any small bits of bone, skin, or vegetables.
7. Place the broth into containers and freeze them. Make sure that you do leave some space in the containers because the broth will expand as it freezes.

This is a great drink to have every day, or you can use it to cook with. This will make a huge batch of chicken broth however, the exact number of servings or ounces will depend on the size of your Crock Pot.

Chicken Pot Pie Stew

Serves: 4
Ingredients

- 1 ½ lbs boneless skinless chicken thighs
- 2 onions, diced finely
- 2 cups sliced celery
- ¾ cup blanched almond flour
- 1 cup chicken stock (optional)

Method

1. Chop the onions and the celery.
2. Place the chicken in the bottom of your Crock Pot and then top the chicken with the chopped up vegetables.
3. Add in the chicken stock and place the lid on the Crock Pot.
4. Cook on low heat for 6 to 8 hours.
5. Once the chicken is done cooking, carefully remove the thighs from the Crock Pot and place them on a plate.
6. Shred them with two forks and then return the shredded meat to the Crock Pot.
7. Stir well before serving.

Baked Chicken With Vegetables

Serves: 1

Ingredients

- 1 whole chicken breast
- 1 bell pepper
- 1 onion
- 1 mushroom
- 2 bacon slices

Method

1. Season your chicken breast with salt and pepper or any season of your choice. Or you can leave it plain.
2. Cut the bell pepper, onion, and mushrooms into pieces that are all about the same size.
3. Place the chicken on a piece of foil and top the chicken with vegetables.
4. Place the bacon on top of the vegetables.
5. Fold the foil into a packet and place it in the Crock Pot.
6. Place the lid on the Crock Pot and cook on low for 6 to 8 hours.

You can make more than one pocket if desired, in fact you can fill the Crock Pot with packets, just make sure that you are leaving one inch of space at the top of the Crock Pot.

Moroccan Chicken

Serves: 3

Ingredients

- 3 chicken breasts,
- A splash of chicken broth
- 8 ounces of broccoli florets
- The spices of your choice (red pepper, salt, black pepper, cumin, or cinnamon, etc.)
- A handful of raisins

Method

1. Place the chicken breasts in the bottom of your Crock Pot followed by the broccoli.
2. Sprinkle the raisins into the Crock Pot and then add in the spices that you want to use. If you are using cinnamon you will want to add in a lot.
3. Toss in the splash of chicken broth.
4. Place the lid on the Crock Pot and cook on low heat for 6 to 8 hours.
5. After the chicken is done cooking, remove it from the Crock Pot and place it on a plate.
6. Using two forks shred the chicken and place it back into the Crock Pot.
7. Stir well and serve hot.

Chicken Taco Soup

Serves: 4 to 6

Ingredients

- 2 cans of Rotel
- 1 (15 ounce) can of tomato sauce
- 1 cup of your favorite salsa
- 4 boneless skinless chicken breasts
- Vegetables of your choice

Optional:

- Taco seasoning

Method

1. Place the chicken breasts in the bottom of the crockpot and cook on high heat for 2 hours.
2. After the chicken has cooked for 2 hours, remove it from the Crock Pot and rinse it off with cool water. Shred the chicken.
3. You may find that there are white slimy bits in your Crock Pot. If so, simply rinse the Crock Pot out.
4. Place the chicken as well as all of the rest of the ingredients into the Crock Pot. Stir well and turn on low heat.
5. Place the lid on the Crock Pot and cook for 4 to 6 hours.
6. This is great served with a dollop of sour cream and a sprinkle of cheddar cheese.

Chicken Curry

Serves: 4 to 6

Ingredients

- 2 cans of coconut milk
- Red curry paste
- Mixed vegetables (bell peppers, eggplant, broccoli, bamboo shoots and onions, etc.)
- 4 to 6 boneless skinless chicken breasts
- Seasonings of your choice (lemongrass, red pepper flakes, fish sauce, cilantro, and Thai basil, etc.)

Method

1. Slice the chicken breasts and cut up the vegetables.
2. Open up your cans of coconut milk.
3. Add two tablespoons of the red curry paste as well as any seasonings and stir until it is completely blended with the thick coconut milk.
4. Once the mixture is completely combined, place it in your Crock Pot.
5. Add in the chicken and vegetables, then cook on low heat for 6 to 8 hours.
6. After the chicken is done cooking, remove it from the Crock Pot and place it on a plate.
7. Shred the chicken using two forks and then place it back into the Crock Pot. Stir well.
8. This is a great dish to serve over rice.

Chicken Soup

Serves: 2

Ingredients

- 1 lb chicken thighs
- 2 onions, chopped
- 2 bunches of celery, chopped
- 2 cups chicken broth

Method

1. Place all of the ingredients into the Crock Pot. Stir.
2. Place the lid on the Crock Pot and cook on low heat for 5 to 6 hours.
3. Once the soup has finished cooking, remove the chicken thighs and place them on a plate.
4. Pull the meat off of the bone and shred it.
5. Place the shredded chicken back in the Crock Pot and stir. Serve hot.

Baked Chicken Legs

Ingredients
- 6 drumsticks
- 2 tbsp melted butter, bacon fat, coconut oil, or ghee
- 2 tbsp your favorite spice blend

Method
1. Pat your drumsticks dry using a paper towel and then place them in your Crock Pot.
2. Brush the drumsticks with the fat that you are using and then sprinkle them with the seasoning blend.
3. Place the lid on the Crock Pot and cook the chicken legs on low heat for 6 to 8 hours.

How to create a delicious spice blend:
- 2 tbsp rosemary salt
- 1 tbsp onion powder
- 1 tbsp garlic powder
- 1 tsp black pepper
- ½ tbsp paprika

Place all of the spices in a bowl and mix well.

Broccoli and Mushroom Chicken Casserole

Serves: 4 to 6

Ingredients

- 1 head of broccoli
- 8 ounces of your favorite mushrooms
- 4 boneless skinless chicken breasts
- 1 can of coconut milk
- 1 tsp curry powder

Method

1. Mix all the ingredients into the Crock Pot. Stir well.
2. Cook it on low heat for 4 to 6 hours.
3. Serve and enjoy.

Pork

Tender Pork Cutlets

Ingredients
- 5 to 6 pork chops
- ½ cup almond flour
- ¼ cup arrowroot powder (you can also use tapioca flour)
- 2 tbsp coconut oil, bacon fat, or ghee
- 1 egg, beaten

Method
1. Place the egg in one dish, and in a separate dish mix the almond flour and the arrowroot powder. Stir the flour to ensure that it is completely mixed.
2. Dip the pork chops in the egg and then dip it in the flour mixture ensuring that both sides are coated evenly.
3. Repeat this process for all of the pork chops.
4. Place the pork chops into your Crock Pot and cook them on low for about 2 hours.
5. Flip them over.
6. Cook for another 2 hours on low.
7. Serve and enjoy.

Tropical Pork Roast

Serves: 8 to 10

Ingredients

- 1 (4 lbs) pork shoulder roast
- 2 red bell peppers, diced
- 2 cups fresh diced pineapple
- 1 can coconut milk
- 3 tbsp chives, basil, and oregano mixed

Method

1. Turn your Crock Pot on. Choose the low heat setting. Place your roast in your Crock Pot and then add in the red bell pepper as well as the diced pineapple.
2. Sprinkle the mixed herbs over the roast and then pour in the coconut milk.
3. Place the lid on the Crock Pot and cook for 7 hours.
4. When the roast is done cooking, use two forks to shred the meat while it is still in the Crock Pot.
5. Reduce the heat to keep warm and allow it to continue cooking for 1 more hour.

Spicy Pork Shoulder

Serves: 4 to 6

Ingredients

- 1 (4 lb) boneless pork shoulder
- 10 cloves of garlic cut in half
- 3 ⅓ cups canned diced tomatoes
- 1 cup beef broth
- 1 tbsp ground chipotle powder

Optional:

- ½ tbsp chili powder
- 1 tsp ground cumin
- Salt and pepper to taste

Method

1. Cut small slits in the pork shoulder using a sharp knife (make 20 small slits).
2. In each of these slits, stuff the halved garlic cloves.
3. Rub salt and pepper on both sides of the pork shoulder.
4. Place your pork shoulder in your Crock Pot.
5. Add the 3 cups of diced tomatoes, the beef broth, and the ground cumin to the Crock Pot.
6. Place the lid on the Crock Pot and select the high setting.
7. Allow the pork shoulder to cook for 6 hours. If you want it to cook longer choose the low setting.
8. When the meat is finished cooking, remove it from the Crock Pot and place it on your cutting board.
9. Take all of the liquid from your Crock Pot and place it in a measuring cup.
10. Using two forks, shred the pork shoulder.
11. Place the shredded pork back into the Crock Pot.
12. Add the chipotle powder, the cumin and the chili powder if you are using it. Mix well.
13. Place 1 ½ cups of the liquid, which you removed back into the Crock Pot as well as rest of the tomatoes. Mix.
14. Choose the keep warm setting. Serve hot when you are ready to eat.

Pork and Apple Hash

Serves: 4

Ingredients

- 2 lbs ground pork (you can also use ground sausage)
- 3 apples, cored and diced
- 6 cups chopped onions

Method

1. Break the ground pork into small bits.
2. Place all the ingredients into the Crock Pot. Mix well.
3. Place the lid on the Crock Pot and cook on low heat for 6 to 8 hours.
4. Serve and enjoy.

Pork Belly

Serves: 6 to 8

Ingredients

- 3 lbs pork belly
- 3 sprigs of rosemary that has been chopped finely
- 1 tsp fennel
- Zest from 1 lemon
- 1 tbsp coconut oil
- Salt and pepper

Method

1. Use a paper towel to pat the pork belly skin dry.
2. Place the coconut oil, lemon zest, fennel, as well as the salt and pepper in a small bowl. Mix well.
3. Rub the coconut oil mixture over the entire pork belly.
4. Place the pork belly in your Crock Pot fat side up and then place the lid on.
5. Cook on low heat for up to 10 hours or high heat for up to 6 hours.

Italian Delight

Serves: 2

Ingredients

- 1 lb Italian sausage
- 1 tomato, chopped
- 2 handfuls of spinach
- 2 tbsp Italian seasoning

Method

1. Place all of the ingredients except for the spinach in the Crock Pot and cook on low for up to 6 hours.
2. About 20 minutes before you are going to serve the dish, stir in the spinach and then allow the cooking process to finish.

Crock Pot Roast With Chimichurri

Serves: 4 to 6

Ingredients

- 1 (3 lbs) boneless pork roast
- 4 tbsp EVOO (extra virgin olive oil), divided
- 1 onion, sliced
- 1 Chimichurri recipe (to follow this one)

Method

1. Place your roast in your Crock Pot.
2. Take 2 tablespoons of the EVOO and drizzle it over the roast. Sprinkle salt and pepper on the roast if desired.
3. Place the lid on the Crock Pot and set the heat to high.
4. After the roast has cooked on high heat for 4 hours, add in the onions. Place the vegetables around the roast but not on top.
5. Drizzle with the remaining EVOO.
6. Place the lid on the Crock Pot and continue to cook for an additional 2 hours.
7. Drizzle chimichurri sauce over the roast and vegetables before serving.

Chimichurri Sauce

Ingredients

- 1 cup fresh parsley, chopped
- 3 cloves of garlic
- ½ cup EVOO
- 2 tbsp lemon juice
- ¼ tsp Cayenne Pepper

Method

1. Place all of your ingredients into your blender and blend until the parsley is small bits.
2. Drizzle over your roast.

Citrus Pulled Pork In The Crock Pot

Serves: 8 to 10

Ingredients

- 5 lbs pork butt
- 2 tbsp sea salt
- Zest and juice from 1 orange, lemon, and lime
- 4 strips of thick bacon

Method

1. Rub the pork butt with the salt and then place the pork butt in the Crock Pot.
2. Add the lemon, orange, and lime juice and zest.
3. Top the pork butt with the bacon.
4. Add in one cup of water and place the lid on the Crock Pot.
5. Choose the low setting and cook for 12 hours.
6. Once the pork has cooked, remove it from the Crock Pot and shred it using two forks.
7. Pour 2 to 3 cups of the liquid from the Crock Pot over the pork. You can serve this in lettuce wraps or top it with some avocado.

Kalua Pork

Serves: 8 to 10

Ingredients

- 5 lbs pork shoulder roast
- 1 tsp salt and pepper(for each of the sides of the roast)
- 3 tbsp liquid smoke
- 1 ½ cups chicken broth
- 1 head of cabbage

Method

1. Mix the salt and the pepper in a small bowl.
2. Rub the salt and pepper mixture on all the sides of the roast.
3. Place the roast in the Crock Pot with the fat side facing up.
4. Place the liquid smoke and the chicken broth in the Crock Pot.
5. Place the lid on the Crock Pot and cook on low heat for 8 hours.
6. After the meat is finished cooking, remove it from the Crock Pot and shred it using two forks.
7. Place the pork back into the Crock Pot and then shred the cabbage.
8. Place the cabbage in the Crock Pot and cook for about 15 minutes or until the cabbage is tender. Serve hot.

Short Ribs

Serves: 6 to 8

Ingredients
- 4 lbs short ribs
- ¼ cup balsamic vinegar
- 4 whole dates
- 1 (14 ounce) can of tomato sauce
- 1 sprig of rosemary

Method
1. Place the short ribs in a skillet on the stovetop over medium to high heat.
2. Brown the short ribs and then place them in the Crock Pot.
3. Add the ¼ cup of balsamic vinegar, the tomato sauce, the whole dates, and the rosemary to the Crock Pot.
4. Place the lid on the Crock Pot and set it on low.
5. Cook the ribs for 6 hours before serving.

Pork Roast

Serves: 6 to 8

Ingredients

- 1 (4 lb) pork butt
- Juice of 1 lemon
- Juice of 1 lime
- 1 cup salsa (make sure that it only contains Ketogenic approved foods)
- Spices (1 tablespoon of cumin, salt, garlic powder, pepper, 1 teaspoon of cayenne, 1 teaspoon of coriander, etc.)

Method

1. Cut the pork but into 6 large chunks (some people may tell you to cut the fat off but it is better not to if you are trying to reach the state of Ketosis).
2. Coat the chunks of pork with garlic powder as well as salt and pepper if you are using it.
3. Place the pork into your Crock Pot and then add in the lemon and lime juice as well as the salsa. Add in the other spices that you want to use.
4. Place the lid on the Crock Pot and select the low setting.
5. Cook for 6 hours.
6. After the meat is finished cooking, use two forks to shred it.

Pulled Pork

Serves: 4 to 6
Ingredients
- 1 (3 lb) pork shoulder
- ½ tsp garlic powder
- 2 cups low sodium chicken broth
- 1 tsp salt
- 3 tsp ground cumin

Method
1. Place the pork shoulder into the Crock Pot.
2. Mix the garlic powder, salt, and cumin in a small bowl.
3. Sprinkle half of the spice mixture on the top of the Crock Pot and then turn the pork over and sprinkle the rest of the spice mixture on the pork.
4. Pour the chicken broth into the Crock Pot and then place the lid on the Crock Pot.
5. Select the low setting and cook the roast for 8 hours.
6. When the meat is done, shred it with two forks and then serve it with your favorite side dishes or on lettuce wraps.

Apple Tenderloin

Serves: 4 to 6

Ingredients

- 4 Gala Apples
- 1 (2 lb) pork tenderloin
- Nutmeg

Optional:

- 2 tbsp honey

Method

1. Core the apples and then slice them.
2. Place the apple slices in your Crock Pot in a single layer. Do not add more than one single layer.
3. Sprinkle the apples with nutmeg.
4. Cut slits into the tenderloin and then cut the tenderloin in half so that it will easily fit into the Crock Pot.
5. Place another layer of apples on top of the tenderloin. Sprinkle the apples with nutmeg. Drizzle with honey if you are using it.
6. Place the lid on the Crock Pot and choose the low setting.
7. Allow to cook for 6 to 8 hours.

Fish

Moonfish

Serves: 4
Ingredients
- 4 leaves from collard greens
- 4 fillets of Opah
- Salt
- 2 tbsp coconut oil

Method
1. Blanch your greens for no more than a couple of seconds and then lay them flat.
2. Cut the tough end off and then place one fillet in the middle of each of the leaves.
3. Use the salt to season the fish and add ½ of a tablespoon of coconut oil to each fillet.
4. Place the fish in your Crock Pot and cook on low heat for 4 hours.
5. If you do not like Opah or have access to it, that is totally fine. You can use this recipe with any fish of your choice however, Opah works well because it is so moist.

Poached Fish

Serves: 1
Ingredients

- Any fish of your choice, as long as it is white
- 1 can of coconut milk
- Salt and pepper

Method

1. Place the coconut milk in the Crock Pot with the fish.
2. Place the lid on the Crock Pot and cook on low heat for 4 hours.
3. Season with salt and pepper

Salmon Burgers

Serves: 2 to 4

Ingredients

- 2 cans of wild salmon that have been drained
- 2 tbsp coconut flour
- 3 eggs
- Shredded coconut, unsweetened

Method

1. Mix the salmon with 2 of the eggs as well as the coconut flour. If you want to add any spices, this is the point that you should do so.
2. Form the mixture into 4 evenly sized patties.
3. Place the shredded coconut in a shallow dish. Place the last egg in a second shallow dish and whisk it well.
4. Dip each of the patties in the egg ensuring that they are completely coated. Then place them in the shredded coconut completely coating them
5. Fry the patties in coconut oil for one minute on both sides and then place them in the Crock Pot.
6. Place the lid on the Crock Pot and cook for 4 hours on low heat.

Catfish

Serves: 1

Ingredients

- 1 catfish fillet
- Coconut oil
- Your favorite catfish seasoning, cajun is amazing
- Juice of ½ lemon
- A sprinkle of paprika powder

Method

1. Dip the fillet in the lemon juice and then sprinkle the seasoning and the paprika powder over it.
2. Melt the coconut oil in your Crock Pot and then add in the catfish.
3. Cook on low heat for 4 hours.
4. Serve with your favorite sides.

Vegetarian

A Bit About Vegetarianism and The Ketogenic Diet

If you want to reach the state of ketosis, you are going to have to ingest a large amount of fat. Most of the time, when a person is following the Ketogenic diet the fat is going to come from animal sources. It is for this reason that animal-based foods and the Ketogenic diet go perfectly together.

However, that is not to say that there are not those out there that do not eat food that comes from animals that want to follow the Ketogenic diet.

Dairy can be controversial when it comes to vegetarians. However, for those that do include dairy and eggs in their diet, these foods will help you reach a state of ketosis.

Eggs are going to provide your body with the healthy fats as will milk and cheeses. You can also add plenty of heavy cream to your coffee in the mornings because it is going to provide you with plenty of fat and little to no carbohydrates.

The problem that many vegetarians face, however, is that they do not know how to replace animal fat with vegetables. You see, as we discussed early on in this book, this diet contains a huge amount of animal fat. However, vegetarians will eat a huge amount of vegetables and berries.

The good news is that there are plenty of ways for you to add healthy fats to your diet without adding a bunch of animal products. For example, nuts such as macadamia nuts or almonds are a great way to add healthy fats to your diet.

Avocados are going to provide you monounsaturated fat as well as plenty of vitamins and nutrients. While it does contain some carbohydrates, it is in the form of fiber which is going to help with digestive health. The carbohydrates in the avocado are not going to affect ketosis like other carbohydrates will.

All things coconut are also going to help you get the amount of fat that you will need in your diet. You can use coconut oil, which can actually be taken by the spoonful, coconut cream, coconut milk, and so forth.

If you are still unable to get the amount of fat that you need in your diet since fruits and vegetables contain no fat, turn to oil. Coconut oil is going to provide you with the best fat, however, you can also use EVOO, Avocado oil, butter, or Macadamia oil.

Vegetables are going to contain more carbohydrates than fatty meats. Because vegetarians must rely on large amounts of fruits and vegetables, you must be very careful to ensure that you are not overdoing it on the carbohydrates.

Try to eat cruciferous vegetables or leafy greens. Cook them in a fat source such as coconut oil or make a salad out of them and drizzle them with EVOO. When it comes to fruit, you will have to be very careful as well. No more bananas. Instead, you will want to eat berries such as blackberries, strawberries, blueberries, or raspberries. However, these should be eaten in moderation because they do contain a lot of sugar.

In short, it is very possible for a vegetarian to follow the Ketogenic diet but it is going to take a lot of work. It is going to be harder for a vegetarian to follow the Ketogenic diet and to reach the state of ketosis because of the large amounts of fruits and vegetables that they have to eat as well as the very little amount of fat that is in their diet.

The majority of the side dishes in this book are vegetarian as are the desserts, however, I also want to provide you with some recipes just for you.

Collard Greens

Serves: 4

Ingredients

- 1 bunch of collard greens
- 6 garlic cloves
- ¼ tsp of salt
- 2 tbsp EVOO (Extra Virgin Olive Oil) or coconut oil

Method

1. Rinse the collard leaves and pat them dry.
2. Cut the tough center stem out and then continue to cut the leaves in half.
3. Stack 5 or 6 of the leaves together and tightly roll them up. Cut the rolls into strips that are about ¼ of an inch wide.
4. Try to keep the strips together if possible and then cut them in half lengthwise. Repeat this process until all of the leaves have been cut.
5. Use your mortar and pestle to smash the garlic together with the salt. If you do not have a mortar and pestle, you can use a garlic press or simply mince the garlic finely.
6. Place the oil in the Crock Pot followed by the greens. Sprinkle the garlic and salt over the greens and then place the lid on the Crock Pot.
7. Cook on low heat for 2 hours.
8. The greens are going to reduce in size by about ½ by the time they are done. Make sure that you do not continue sautéing them after they have become bright green because they will begin to get dark which means they are overcooked.
9. Serve them as soon as they are finished cooking.

Desserts/ Snacks

Mug Cake

Serves: 1 to 4, depending on the size of mug

Ingredients

- 1 banana
- 1 egg
- 1 ½ tsp almond butter
- 2 tbsp unsweetened cocoa powder
- 1 tbsp coconut cream

Method

1. Place all of the ingredients (except for the coconut cream) in a blender and mixing well.
2. Coat your mug with coconut oil and then pour the batter from the blender into the mug.
3. Fill the mugs and place them into the Crock Pot.
4. Fill the Crock Pot 1/2 of the way up the side of the mugs with water and cook on low for 1 hour.
5. Top with coconut cream.

Almond Butter and Banana bread

Serves: 4 to 6
Ingredients
- ½ cup almond butter
- ½ tsp baking soda
- 1 egg
- 2 dates
- 1 banana, mashed

Method
1. Place the almond butter into your blender as well as the egg, dates, and baking soda. Blend until completely smooth or for about 1 minute.
2. Add the banana to the ingredients in the blender and continue to blend until the banana is completely incorporated.
3. Use coconut oil to grease your bread pan or line it, then pour the mixture into the pan.
4. Place the pan in the in the Crock Pot and cook for 4 hours on low heat.

You can also add: Blueberries, almond slivers, vanilla, coconut flakes, or cinnamon.

Side Dishes

Crispy Sweet and Sour Brussels Sprouts

Serves: 4 to 6
Ingredients

- 2 tbsp coconut oil or ghee
- 1 tbsp maple syrup
- ½ tbsp fish sauce
- ½ tbsp lemon juice
- 2 lbs fresh Brussels sprouts

Optional:

- Salt
- A bit of hot sauce

Method

1. Cut each of the Brussels sprouts in half and then place them in your Crock Pot.
2. Melt the coconut oil or ghee. Drizzle the melted oil or ghee over the Brussels sprouts and toss them using your hands to ensure they are completely coated. Sprinkle salt over the Brussels sprouts.
3. Cook on low heat for 8 hours.
4. While they are cooking, mix the fish sauce, maple syrup, lemon juice, and the hot sauce if you are using it.
5. After the Brussels sprouts are done cooking, add the sauce into the Crock Pot and toss before serving.

Garlic aioli (to dip the fries in)

Ingredients
- 2 cloves of garlic
- 2 egg yolks
- ¾ cup olive oil
- Juice from ½ lemon
- A pinch of salt

Method
1. Place all of the ingredients into a blender.
2. Turn the blender on low and begin adding the olive oil slowly until you reach the thickness that you desire.
3. Dip fries in the sauce.

Baked Vegetables in the Crock Pot

Serves: 4

Ingredients

- 1 head of broccoli, cut into florets
- ½ lb Brussels sprouts, halved
- 3 tbsp coconut oil, melted
- Garlic powder
- Salt and pepper

Method

1. Place all of the vegetables in a large bowl and pour the coconut oil over them.
2. Toss to ensure all of the vegetables are coated.
3. Place the vegetables in the Crock Pot.
4. Sprinkle with the garlic powder and the salt and pepper.
5. Place the lid on the Crock Pot and cook them on low heat for 4 hours.

Crispy Veggies

Serves: 4 to 6

Ingredients

- 3 cups of your favorite vegetables (bell peppers, Brussels sprouts, eggplant, red onions, or asparagus, etc.), cut into pieces that are about the same size.
- 1 tbsp olive oil
- Salt and pepper
- Garlic powder

Method

1. Place all of the vegetables in a gallon sized Zip Lock bag.
2. Pour the olive oil into the bag with the vegetables and close the bag.
3. Shake the bag until the vegetables are completely coated with the olive oil.
4. Place the vegetables into the Crock Pot and then sprinkle the garlic powder, salt, and pepper over the vegetables.
5. Place the lid on the Crock Pot and cook on low heat for 4 hours.

Oven Roasted Brussels Sprouts in the Crock Pot

Serves: 3 to 5
Ingredients

- 1 ½ pounds of Brussels Sprouts
- 3 tbsp EVOO (extra virgin olive oil)
- ¾ tsp salt
- ½ tsp pepper

Method

1. Cut the ends off of the Brussels sprouts and then pull any of the outer leaves off that are yellow. Half the Brussels sprouts.
2. Place the Brussels sprouts, the salt, pepper, and the EVOO in a large bowl and toss until the spouts are completely coated.
3. Place the sprouts in the Crock Pot. Cook them on low heat for 6 hours.
4. Season with salt and serve.

Chili Lime Acorn Squash

Serves: 6 to 8

Ingredients

- 2 acorn squash
- 1 tbsp coconut oil or ghee
- 1 tbsp lime juice
- 1 tsp chili powder

Method

1. Melt the coconut oil or the ghee and then mix in the chili powder and the lime juice.
2. Cut the acorn squash into wedges and then place the wedges into the Crock Pot.
3. Drizzle the oil mixture over the acorn squash wedges.
4. Place the lid on the Crock Pot and then cook on low heat for 6 hours.

Conclusion

There you have it! I hope that this book has helped you learn all about the Ketogenic diet, how you can use your Crock Pot to ensure that you are able to stick to the diet, and I hope that you have found plenty of recipes that you and your family will enjoy.

Sticking to the Ketogenic diet is very easy when you follow the information that you have been given in this book. It is even easier when you have tons of recipes at your fingertips so that when mealtime comes, you don't find yourself confused or trying to figure out what you should eat.

The Ketogenic diet can provide everyone with many benefits, from weight loss, to a clearer mind, to better focus, and so much more. I hope that with the information that you have learned in this book, you are able to experience those benefits and live a healthy happy life.

Made in the USA
Las Vegas, NV
28 September 2023

78274994R00063